Why Men Depress Women

by

Dr. Edward M. Waring

DORRANCE
PUBLISHING CO
EST. 1920
PITTSBURGH, PENNSYLVANIA 15236

Dorrance Publishing Co
585 Alpha Drive
Suite 103
Pittsburgh, PA 15238
Visit our website at *www.dorrancebookstore.com*

ISBN: 978-1-4809-3311-8
eISBN: 978-1-4809-3334-7

Dedicated to Alicia

Women experience depression when they lose hope of developing or maintaining a close, confiding relationship with a man.

Chapter One
Women

One in four women will experience a clinically significant mood disorder in their lifetime. Some have suggested this figure may be as high as four out of ten. Women are at higher risk for most types of depression. A consistent finding is a female-to-male ratio of two to one for serious depression. Most of these women will say that their depression was triggered or prolonged by problems in their marriages. A relationship between being depressed and being married but miserable has been established.

While we know that mood disorders are more common in women than men, we don't have a precise explanation. Perhaps a possible explanation is that women have to cope with men. This rather simple reason does not exclude other possible vulnerabilities such as having a family history of mood disorders, biological risk factors such as hormonal changes, or perhaps social and cultural factors.

One should also remember that one in ten men will experience depression in their lifetime and many more will experience alcohol abuse. Any understanding of why women are more likely to experience mood disorders must also explain why six out of ten don't experience depression.

Genetic, Biochemical, and Hormonal Factors

There is some evidence of a genetic component in some types of depression. Depression does run in families from generation to generation. Some researchers have suggested a sex-linked risk for certain mood disorders. However, such theories have not received consistent support. We have no consistent data, which could tell us what specifically is inherited by women that would make them more vulnerable to mood disorders. One could say

1

that currently there is no genetic theory to explain the gender difference in depression.

We have been described as the Prozac generation. In truth the antidepressant medications have been around for approaching fifty years. Since these medications work in some people with depression, researchers have suggested that the actions of these medications may explain the cause of some mood disorders. Antidepressants work by changing the way neurotransmitters like serotonin and norepinephrine work in the central nervous system. Initially, researchers thought the drugs acted by increasing the neurotransmitters in the synapses, the spaces between neurons or nerve cells in the brain. However, these changes occur within twenty-four hours after the drugs are given, while the antidepressants take up to two to four weeks to work. Next, researchers focused on changes to the receptors on the cell surface, which serotonin and norepinephrine occupy. Now, researchers are focusing on subsequent changes within the nerves that are triggered by receptor occupancy. These changes within the cell may be linked to genetic susceptibility. The problem is that these studies do not explain what triggers these biological changes in the first place. So, although we have the belief that some depressions may have a biochemical factor, our research has left us with more questions than answers.

Hormonal Changes
Mood changes in some women are associated with menstrual periods, pregnancy, childbirth, menopause and steroid metabolism. However, since most women experience some of the above experiences without mood disorders we need to understand what hormonal changes are different in women who experience depression.

Considerable experience and research has implicated progesterone, estrogen and cortisol as playing some role in the development of depression. The cortisol suppression test was developed as a marker for depression but was found to be neither sensitive nor specific.

Why these hormones should precipitate depression in some women and not others is unknown.

In summary, considerable research has led to a belief that at least some depression is biological in origin and there is no doubt that antidepressants and ECT do improve symptoms of depression in many women. But, the specifics of how genetic, biochemical and hormonal factors precipitate depression remains unknown.

Sociocultural Factors

Mood disorders have been found to be associated with a wide variety of sociocultural risk factors in some research and not others. Mood disorders can occur at any age from childhood to the elderly. Poverty would seem on the surface to be associated with low mood but, in fact, it is loss of wealth or status that is more frequently associated with depression. A vulnerability does seem to exist in Western culture between women with young children, low income and mood disorders but this also seems to be mediated by the quality of the woman's relationship.

Divorce, separation and abandonment of marital status have often been associated with mood disorders but recently an awareness that being married, but miserable, is different from a successful marriage has decreased the specificity of marital status. One should also keep in mind that long before couples actually separate or divorce the psychological bond may be over, with resultant joy for some women who are leaving poor relationships, or despair for those who want the relationship to continue. There is much popular literature on aspects of women's roles in society, which may be diminished by various types of repression and bias but as real as their concerns are, a specific relationship to mood disorders has not been found.

It is perhaps surprising then, to realize that in spite of considerable research in both biology and epidemiology, that we don't have a clearer understanding of why mood disorders are more common in women. Hopefully, our closer examination of the role of interpersonal attachments will add some missing pieces to this puzzle.

Chapter Two
Depression

Depression is a pervasive and persistent lowering of mood, which lasts for weeks and usually months without response to the usual occasional joys of day-to-day living.

Depression is NOT unhappiness, sadness or grief, although some of the symptoms experienced are similar. Unhappiness is more of an attitude that something specific doesn't please you. Unfortunately, if that something specific is your entire life, then unhappiness can be a risk factor for depression. Always (ALWAYS) unhappy people often have personality traits of introspection, neuroticism, sensitivity, self-preoccupation and are vulnerable to mood disorders. BUT, being unhappy for a few days or feeling sad for a few hours is normal and not a mood disorder. Sadness is a feeling we all experience but frequently express differently (i.e., men cry when feeling sad, women cry when feeling frustrated). Sadness, is surprisingly, not the feeling most expressed by women with mood disorders (i.e., down, blue, numb, etc.). Grief is a different story. Grief is a normal human response to loss. The grieving process, usually lasting six to eight weeks, takes different forms in different cultures but for the individual involves feelings of shock, denial or disbelief followed by sadness and preoccupation with thoughts of the lost loved one, accompanied by some level of social withdrawal.

Most of you will have experienced the above and will recognize that normal grief has a striking similarity to depression. In fact, abnormal grief often leads to depression.

What is the difference between normal and abnormal grief? In abnormal grief the sufferer does not experience, or express the normal conscious mixed feelings we have about people we feel close to and, as a result, these negative feelings are turned against ourselves. Whose theory is this? Freud, in 1918, wrote a brilliant short article about mourning (normal grief) and melancholia (depression). Although Freud's other work about human sexuality has been controversial for the past two decades, nobody seriously disputes his theory of grief and depression.

Let me give you an example. Two sisters' mother dies. One sister says she was a saint to put up with their father. The second sister says she was a good mother but she was annoyed she put up with him. Which sister is prone to depression?

You're right, the first sister might develop an abnormal grief reaction in which she would say, "I feel guilty that I was such a poor daughter in not standing up to my father." For her, the mixed feelings of love and annoyance expressed by her sister are, for some reason, unacceptable to the first sister.

So, mood disorders differ from normal grief reactions in severity, length and content, particularly issues of worthlessness, guilt and suicidality. The mood disorder is NOT sadness but an inability to enjoy anything. Feelings of hopelessness, helplessness, pessimism, or prolonged insomnia, anorexia, weight loss, loss of libido, low energy and poor concentration follow. Sometimes thoughts can be ruminative about past sins or even delusions that one has cancer or senility. Those of you interested in reading the full description of mood disorders will find reading the American Psychiatric Association's DSM IV instructive. For our purposes we will be exploring the relationship of Dysthymia (longer duration, milder symptoms) and Major Affective Disorder (present two weeks, with severe symptoms) to aspects of relationship attachment.

So, for the rest of our discussion, we will be exploring why men cause women to develop Dysthymia and Major Depressive Disorders.

Chapter Three
Lose Hope

Every day we read in the newspapers, or watch on television, more news of celebrity marriages breaking up, of episodes of domestic violence and murder. Yet young people today continue to plan to marry and hope their relationship will be a good one. Some years ago we did a study of married couples (excluding those already divorced, separated or abandoned) and found that only one in five had a close, confiding relationship.

So, given the evidence that the quality of most marriages is miserable, where does this hope come from and how is this hope lost?

Well, we actually know a great deal about how to develop a good, affectionate attachment. The first rule is to trust your instinctive judgement about who you are attracted to, or fall in love with, because your unconscious has the capacity to make good choices based on past experiences. However, rule two is, don't marry everyone you fall in love with! The second stage of courtship should involve the process of mutual self-disclosure of values, beliefs and goals (the process of getting to know somebody). The third rule is, to spend enough everyday time together to learn if you are compatible, because we like people who are similar and liking is more important than loving in the long run.

Basically, if people followed these three rules, I would have hope that the quality of marriages would improve.

But, as a marital therapist, these are the stories I hear over and over with couples who break the three rules. "I didn't like him at first but he was very persistent." "I wasn't attracted at all but I needed someone because I was so lonely." "In spite of his bad reputation, I just wanted to show my parents." What will these women do after they are married and do find someone attractive (psychologists say we all fall in love three to seven times during our lifespan)?

Rule number two is broken by people who present a persona, or pretend to be someone, in order to be accepted or admired. So, what happens after the wedding, when she reveals she doesn't want any children, in spite of saying she wanted a large family? Without honest self-disclosure during courtship we have no choice about aspects of religion, sexuality, parenting and life goals.

And, finally, how many couples have we known who fight all the time during courtship but hope this will stop after the ceremony?

So, how do these women, who have broken all the rules, lose hope and why are they ambivalent about this hope?

Well, usually in the first year or two, they realize that these men are not going to respect the boundaries of the marriage agreement. They still spend the weekends with their buddies, or spend most of their time with the in-laws, or keep having lunch with that old girlfriend, who makes her feel so jealous. They may give up hope after a year or two.

They may hope that after three or four years the arguments might stop, or the fights may be less upsetting. But, she may lose hope that she can ever influence her husband, or control the situation. Finally, she may lose hope of ever developing a close, confiding relationship.

So, why does losing hope precipitate depression? The answer may go back to the lack of acceptability of the mixed feelings about hope. Hope is part of the human condition but it may have the annoying aspect of allowing us to deny certain realities. What was motivating me to pick a man I disliked? Why did I lack the confidence to reveal my true values? Why did I pretend his drinking would stop after marriage?

So, clinical depression is often triggered by losses where the person consciously feels the loss (the relationship) is perfect, in spite of the more objective reality that the relationship never had a hope of being a close, confiding relationship. The loss only precipitates or triggers depression in the spouse who wants the relationship to continue, or hopes it can be improved. This loss of hope often occurs months or even years before separation or divorce.

Chapter Four
Developing or Maintaining a Relationship

Women may, or may not be, biologically or socio-culturally more prone to losses. Particularly, losses which are associated with relationships and, more specifically, to the loss of hope of developing or maintaining a relationship with a man in marriage, or common law, or just an affectionate attachment.

Bowlby has written persuasively about the influence of early childhood attachments and their problems in relation to adult relationship difficulties. Bowlby's theories are more widely accepted than Freud's and the following is a brief and biased summary.

Basically, Bowlby says that our attachment to our mothers (could also be any nurturing caretaker) in our first year or two is critical to our personality development and adult relationships. At one extreme, total neglect, abuse or abandonment, leaves us with NO hope of developing a close, confiding relationship. A good example would be to explore the backgrounds of prostitutes and their customers, who can only barter for sex for money without even the pretext of a relationship. At the other extreme are mothers who are nurturing, soothing, reliable, affectionate and respect the developing individuality of their daughters who, not surprisingly, have the greatest potential for close adult relationships.

In between are children, who Bowlby described as developing anxious attachments, as a consequence of mothering (or caretaking) that is, at times "good enough" but is inconsistent, tense, or inhibited by worry and apprehension. In my opinion, these are the daughters who develop HOPE of finding a close, confiding relationship because they have had "a little taste" but not enough, to make them feel secure or develop self-esteem and so they look for that consistency elsewhere. So, where do little girls look for closeness if it has been only inconsistently supplied by their mothers? Obviously, as they grow into childhood, such closeness can be derived from mother substitutes such as sisters, girlfriends, aunts, grandmothers, teachers and other role models. But, for many women this hope for closeness, nurturance and affection is turned toward their fathers. Mirroring the situation with their mothers, this hope can be met at extremes of neglectful, absent or abusive men who leave the young women with no hope, or, good-enough fathers who compensate with affection and attention, producing the further hope that romance will lead to the "idealized" close, confiding relationship.

So, in the previous chapter and this one, we have answered the question of which women lose hope of developing a close, confiding relationship. If you wish, these are women who have experienced enough attachment in childhood to hope for more in the future but whose IQ (intimacy quotient or potential) is not high enough to avoid "looking for love in all the wrong places," or, as suggested in the previous chapter, breaking the courtship rules because the need is too great.

However, some of these women will find partners who are good enough to provide a close relationship but their fears of maintaining the relationship may contribute to undermining and losing their partners to separation or divorce, or to abnormal grief reactions. A psychologist, named George Kelly, suggested that these women would construe their partners' behaviors as threatening them with loss of their relationship, such that the women may actually provoke abandonment as a kind of self-fulfilling prophecy. More about this rather complex notion later.

Chapter Five
Intimacy (Closeness)

What is intimacy? Intimate relationships are probably the most important kind of interpersonal relationships. They are felt most deeply. They provide a unique sense of attachment and belonging. Marital intimacy is not just the sum of two independently acting individuals but is a mix of two personalities, which as a dyad has qualities not present in the actions of the isolated spouses. Erikson (1950) suggests that the development of intimacy is the major psychosocial task of young adulthood. The behavioral aspect of intimacy is predictability; the emotional aspect is a feeling of closeness; the cognitive aspect is understanding through self-disclosure; and the attitudinal aspect is commitment.

Intimacy is one of three psychological dimensions, which can describe the quality of interpersonal relationships. "Boundary" and "power" are the other two psychological dimensions. Boundary refers to the couple's relationships in time and space to other individuals and social units. Power refers to the couple's capacity to resolve their conflicting needs and the style they use to resolve such differences.

Intimacy is the dimension, which most determines satisfaction with relationships that endure over time. The development of intimacy is a process which depends on a variety of factors, including 1) childhood attachments; 2) the observation of and experience with one's parents' marriage; 3) one's personality; and 4) experience in personal relationships.

The quantity and quality of intimacy in a couple's relationship at a given point in time can be described by the following eight facets:

1. Conflict resolution — the ease with which differences of opinion is resolved.
2. Affection — the degree to which feelings of emotional closeness are

expressed by the couple.

3. Cohesion — a feeling of commitment to the marriage.
4. Sexuality – the degree to which sexual needs are communicated and fulfilled by the marriage.
5. Identity—the couple's level of self-confidence and self-esteem.
6. Compatibility – the degree to which the couple is able to work and play together comfortably.
7. Autonomy – the success to which the couple gains independence from their families of origin and their offspring.
8. Expressiveness – the degree to which thoughts, beliefs, attitudes, and feelings are shared within the marriage.

I think most readers would agree that having a mother who was sensitive to our needs as an infant, accepting of our behavior, cooperative in our development, and accessible when approached, might enhance our potential for intimacy in our marriages. While accepting that such attachments may be prototypes for adult relationships, the majority of us cannot remember our infancy. The influence of this crucial stage of development remains unconscious. It may also be that the adult who wants to be close with his or her spouse may be motivated by factors, which are independent of earlier attachments.

Jung suggests that whenever we speak of a "psychological relationship" we presuppose one that is "conscious," for there is no such thing as a psychological relationship between two people who are in a state of unconsciousness. There is in all marriages, a considerable degree of partial unconsciousness, especially in the choice of the spouse. Thus, I believe the conscious observation and experience of one's parents' level of intimacy, between the ages of about four to ten, will have a profound influence on one's capacity for intimacy. However, one must also attempt to understand the unconscious tie to the parents and conditions under which it modifies, or prevents conscious choice and influences therapy. Jung suggested that children react much less to what grownups say, than to the imponderables in the surrounding atmosphere. This explanation focuses on the couple's conscious memories of the quality of their parents' intimacy.

What we do remember from the age of three or four is our experience of our mother as a woman, our father as a man, both as parents, and the quality of their marriage. We grew up observing and experiencing a marriage. Paradoxically, the quality and quantity of intimacy in our parents' marriages may have influenced the degree of maternal sensitivity and acceptance we experienced as infants and children. In turn, our parents may have been influenced by their own observation and experience with their parents' level of intimacy. We may also remember sharing our observations and experiences of our parents' marriages with our siblings and our friends. "Why are Mom and Dad always fighting?" "Why do they sleep in separate bedrooms?" "Why does Father drink so much?"

Research on the quality of early attachments demonstrated that the total absence of a mother, or a mother substitute during the first year of life, frequently results in physical, emotional, and intellectual limitations. Where the neglect is profound, the infant can simply fail to thrive in infancy and fail to survive into adulthood. When the neglect is more emotional and no bond develops between infant and mother, many observers believe the seeds are planted for the development of the adult psychopath. This is an individual who is unable to develop intimacy with members of the opposite sex in adulthood because of an almost total absence of the capacity for empathy, understanding, or caring for another individual.

Ethnologists have confirmed these observations on human infants in that severe neglect in many species, both in the laboratory and in natural surroundings, produces an adult who is incapable of mating, parenting, or peer relationships. At this extreme, of total absence of mothering or severe neglect, occurring in the first six months or year of life no bond develops. Erikson suggests that, if the infant survives at all, it survives without the capacity for basic trust—a prime factor in the development of intimacy in adulthood.

Between the ages of one and three, the infant and mother develop an attachment, which is based more on the quality of the mothering and temperament of the infant. At first glance, it may appear ludicrous to consider that hereditary factors can influence an adult personality's potential for intimacy. However, the innate individual equipment of physique, temperament, and general intellectual capacity do set limits on constitutional endowment on the highly complex abilities of the adult to develop intimacy. The mother can also vary, from abuse and neglect at one extreme, to what Winnicott has termed "good-enough mothering," which I already described. The quality of maternal care varies from these extremes to the more common inconsistency, or over-involvement, we all may have experienced.

I refer to this next stage as attachment because it is dependent on the quality of the relationship. Most adults can identify the qualitative tone of this period, even if they cannot put it into words and remember specific instances.

Thus, if any kind of mothering or caretaking occurs in the first six months to a year, a bond is formed, which is intact irrespective of the quality of the mothering. But in the second stage, where an attachment is formed, the quality of the mothering is perceived by the infant and colors an unconscious affective tone. As examples, Bowlby describes those infants who experience "inconsistent mothering" at this time as developing anxious attachment. An infant experiencing a "neglectful" or abusive mother may experience hostile attachment and an infant experiencing an "overprotective mother" may experience a narcissistic attachment. I should like to emphasize, again, that these experiences are largely unconscious and may influence the kinds of unconscious expectations and attitude, which result in poorly understood behaviors in marriage. Spouses may be consistently anxious about the attachment to the spouse, continually hostile toward the spouse, or continually having expectations that the spouse will meet all of their needs, although they cannot say why!

The next major developmental stage with relevance to adult intimacy is between the ages of three and five years. The closeness, which now may develop between a mother and child, is dependent on the actual qualities of their relationship and the verbal action between the two.

There are a number of psychological features at this age, which may have implications for the development of adult intimacy. These include the psychological issue of separation/individualization. This involves the development in the child of a mental representation of the mother. The child maintains this mental image of the mother, even when the child is not in contact with her. A second important part of this phase is the development of different types of abstract thinking in the child described by Piaget. A third feature is children's beginning awareness that they can choose to keep their thoughts, ideas, and feelings to themselves if they wish.

This period is culminated when the child enters school and relationships with siblings, peers, and teachers become important. It is during this time period that the child can consciously begin to remember, observe, and experience the qualitative aspects of his or her parents' relationship. Closeness at this stage is moving away from the unconscious, emotionally perceived experience, depending on the affective quality of the relationship with the mother, to closeness with other figures, which is dependent on self-disclosure of thoughts and feelings that the individual controls. It is at this stage that children develop best friends, with whom they share secrets of their experience, thoughts and feelings, excluding such information from their parents for the first time.

In summary, infants who do not develop a bond with a mother, or maternal figure, would appear to be incapable of developing intimacy as adults. Children who have problems in the period of attachment will often have profound difficulties in development of intimacy in adulthood. Children, who have difficulties with closeness in the latency period, may also have difficulties with closeness as adults.

These observations come mainly from the work of psychoanalysts, ethnologists, and recent research, which has directly studied the development of infants and children. Ideally, an infant who is born to a mother who is sensitive, accepting, cooperative, and accessible will develop a strong bond to the mother. The child will develop a positive attachment and will feel close to the mother during the early phase of childhood. If the child then observes and experiences his parents having an intimate relationship with one another and has the opportunity to develop close relationships with peers, siblings, and teachers, the seeds for development of optimal intimacy have been sown. The next major developmental period is the adolescent's search for identity.

I think that the quality and quantity of intimacy in a marriage constitute the single most important factor in marital satisfaction and family function. Optimal intimacy is associated with the absence of anxiety and depression in both spouses. Optimal intimacy produces a family environment characterized by adaptiveness and cohesion. This operational definition of intimacy was developed in the context of a theory, which attempts to explain why some families have members with emotional disorders and other families do not. If this operational definition of marital intimacy can be measured with reliability and validity, a test of the theory of why men depress women is possible.

Initially, several studies were done to evaluate what facets of marital intimacy needed to be measured. The first study, involved asking couples in the general population what intimacy meant to them. The second study, involved the completion of several self-report questionnaires regarding facets of marriage, to evaluate which elements were associated with marital adjustment. A third study, involved interviewing and videotaping couples with marital discord and nonpsychotic emotional illness and comparing them to couples who were adjusted. Differences that might help us identify intimacy were identified. These studies were completed in the absence of a specific review of other researchers' operational definitions of intimacy, although these were eventually explored. These operational definitions are available to the interested reader in a review by Schaefer and Olson. We developed a standardized, structured interview as well as a self-report questionnaire based on the eight facets of intimacy, which have been mentioned previously but are worth repeating.

1. Conflict resolution — the ease with which differences of opinion is resolved.
2. Affection — the degree to which feelings of emotional closeness are expressed by the couple.
3. Cohesion — a feeling of commitment to the marriage.
4. Sexuality the degree to which sexual needs are communicated and fulfilled by the marriage.
5. Identity – the couple's level of self-confidence and self-esteem.
6. Compatibility – the degree to which the couple is able to work and play together comfortably.
7. Autonomy— the success with which the couple gains independence from their families of origin and their offspring.
8. Expressiveness — the degree to which thoughts, beliefs, attitudes, and feelings are shared within the marriage.

The structured interview, the Victoria Hospital Intimacy Interview (VHII), included ratings on "overall intimacy" and "intimate behavior" observed during the interview. The self-report questionnaire contains a control scale for social desirability. The interview and the questionnaire both have acceptable reliability and validity, which is reported elsewhere.

Why are the operational definition and the measurement instruments important? I think readers are able to evaluate whether my definition of intimacy corresponds to their own ideas about intimacy. The operational definition allows you to evaluate whether some facet included, or some facet excluded, might improve the operational definition.

But, perhaps of more importance, the operational definition can be used to explain intimacy to couples. Each couple is able to judge experientially whether they think they are not as close as they wish to be, and they can objectively compare their level of intimacy to that of other couples. The couple is also able to identify which facets of intimacy in their relationship need greater understanding and which facets are satisfactory. For example, couples in which one or both spouses have psychosomatic symptoms, often have a pattern of high commitment, positive identity, high compatibility and good conflict resolution combined with deficiencies in sexuality, expression of affection, autonomy, and self-disclosure.

These objective measures have also allowed us to develop operational definitions of four types of marital intimacy and their prevalence both in the general population and in specific patient groups. These four types of intimacy are discussed next.

Optimal Intimacy

One in every ten couples who marry will develop optimal intimacy. The spouses come from families characterized by open communication and intimacy. They have had close relationships with parents, siblings, and peers. They know who they are, what they want to do, and who they want to be within relationships.

Such couples are enjoyable to interview and share a sense of humor. Their values, goals and attitudes are so similar that they rarely have differences of opinion. They verbally express respect, caring, loving, and liking. They are committed to their marriage, which is their most important relationship. The couple is actively involved with extended family, friends and community. They communicate in an open, honest and respectful manner and disclose their private thoughts to each other.

Optimally intimate families rarely visit physicians except for serious accidents or illness. Sociologists find such couples dull, traditional, and stereotyped. The media find them boring. Mental health professionals are cynical about their happiness. These responses notwithstanding, the optimally intimate couples show remarkable physical and emotional health and stable family environments.

Adequate Intimacy

Two out of every ten couples develop adequate marital intimacy. Adequate intimacy is neither a statistical nor a cultural norm. Essentially, this type of intimacy involves areas of strength and areas of weakness in the relationship, but weaknesses such as lack of compatibility or difficulties with sexuality are perceived accurately and acknowledged by both, and the strengths outweigh the weaknesses. These couples may attend marital enrichment programs or seek marital counseling for specific problems. Typically, a couple who is very committed, compatible and caring, may have a specific sexual problem or recurrent argument, which they do not understand and they seek professional help. Because of other strengths, these couples do extremely well with professional help, but the majority simply accepts and adjusts to their difficulties.

Pseudo-Intimacy

These couples have more areas of weakness than strength in their intimate relationships, but for a variety of reasons they attempt to make a good impression. Two out of every ten couples who marry develop a pattern of pseudo-intimacy. Although the spouses hunger for intimate love relationships, they settle for the symbols of marital adjustment and the sense of a family. The most commonly seen pattern of pseudo-intimacy is where one spouse, usually the wife, perceives the relationship as lacking in affection and compatibility and feels she does not have a close, confiding relationship with her husband. The husband, however, does not perceive or acknowledge these difficulties. The wife may stay in the relationship for the benefit of the children, for social acceptability, or because of fears or insecurities, but she will seek medical help for symptoms of anxiety or depression.

A second example is a patient with chronic pain who says her marriage is fine, her husband supportive, and they never argue. On close evaluation, one often finds they never argue because they never express themselves; the husband is solicitous, but there is no genuine affection and no sexuality and the couple maintains the façade of marital adjustment through social isolation.

A final example is the pseudo-mutuality of families where the marriage is characterized by pseudo-intimacy. A couple who refuse, or who are unable to perceive their lack of intimacy, may focus criticism, attention or expressed emotion on a child, who may become a scapegoat to maintain the fragile stability of a family.

Deficient or Absent Intimacy

Two out of every ten couples who marry stay together, despite lack of overt closeness between the spouses. Interestingly, the statistical average for marriage in our society, the median couple, is between pseudo-intimacy and deficient intimacy, a far cry from our cultural myths about marriage.

Marriages with deficient intimacy are characterized by open discord, physical abuse, alcoholism, affairs, chronic grudges, alliances with children, and chaotic family life. Although they lack affection, have poor communication, frequent arguments, and poor sexuality, these couples are surprisingly committed and there are moments of joy in the chaotic family life. Physicians become involved with these couples though suicide attempts, alcoholism, venereal disease and antisocial behavior on the part of the children.

Divorce

Three out of every ten couples who marry will separate and/or divorce. Some couples will never develop any closeness and some will lose an attachment, irrespective of their level of intimacy. The couples who recognize they have not made a genuine commitment, as those who married because of a premarital pregnancy or who battle for control, may not develop intimacy. These separations or divorces may allow both an opportunity for counseling, to carefully explore their reasons for marital choice.

Couples who have developed some degree of intimacy present a different problem. There is evidence that the time between the breaking of affectionate ties in the relationship and actual physical separation or divorce is the period of greatest vulnerability for depression and suicide attempts. This period can last longer than two years for many of these couples.

Chapter Six
Self-Disclosure (Confiding)

Self-disclosure is the process of verbally revealing one's thoughts, feelings and beliefs to another person. A psychologist named Sidney Jourard wrote an excellent book called *The Transparent Self*, in which he described self-disclosure and outlined the importance of the process of self-disclosure in the development of relationships. He made the observation that people who do not self-disclose, often seek out professional psychotherapists who they pay to listen to their inner selves.

Self-disclosure is just one aspect of communication but it is vital to the development of relationships. Research shows that women self-disclose more than men and the greatest amount of self-disclosure occurs in marriages. Another psychologist named, Gordon Chelune, who I had the pleasure of working together with in research, is an expert in the measurement of different aspects of self-disclosure. We found that self-disclosure (a verbal process) was the single thread, which explained a person's feeling of closeness in a relationship where the amount of self-disclosure was high, and the self-disclosure was equal between the partners and the self-disclosures were positive in tone and more personal or private.

In summary, self-disclosure is a process in which we get to "know" important aspects of how others think and feel, as well as their beliefs, values and attitudes and even their daydreams, wishes and aspects of their imagination. How then does self-disclosure help us to understand why men depress women? First, you will be interested to know that there are studies of depressed women's marriages, which show low amounts of self-disclosure and/or imbalances of self-disclosure. However, we must go back even earlier to understand why this situation has developed. In previous chapters, we suggested that an underlying motivation for women who are prone to depression was anxious attachment, which may be precipitated by real or imagined loss in early relationships. Thus, the woman hopes for a close relationship, in order to compensate for the loss, but this creates a paradox. The process of honest and open self-disclosure during courtship risks revealing beliefs and values, which may precipitate another loss. For example, if the woman with anxious attachment reveals that she doesn't want to have children, or she doesn't really like sex, or she favors a specific religion, she risks the man deciding that this is not the woman he is looking for and leaves. So, when, or if, the woman who is vulnerable, is attracted to a potential partner she may avoid self-disclosure in order to present a persona, which she believes, will be attractive to her partner. Since there is a great tendency for relationships to be compatible for the level of emotional immaturity, the woman who is fearful of open disclosures is going to be attracted to "the strong, silent type." I wish I had a dollar for the number of times I have heard depressed women say, "He was such a good listener during our romance!" "He seemed to be so in control." What they learn, in retrospect, is that they have chosen a man who does not self-disclose his own thoughts and feelings. The couple often actively colludes in this process of mutual obfuscation, while enjoying the romance. These courtships are often very short, as well, to avoid any unpleasant beliefs, values or feelings to destroy the mirage. Even the marriage ceremony, with choices of religion, family, customs, etc., can be a minefield. The honeymoon, with its forced exposure to day-to-day living, may leave the couple with nothing to say, or begin the process of revealing undisclosed conflicts about sex, children, leisure, relatives and life style. Now comes the low mood and the complaint, "I never knew what he was thinking."

One of the outcomes of the process of self-disclosure is that we learn whether or not our values, beliefs and attitudes are compatible. Compatibility is an important aspect of long-term relationships, because we tend to like people who we construe as similar. In close relationships, one finds that couples like each other as well as respecting and loving. Where there is incompatibility there will be more conflict and conflict will test any couple's capacity for problem solving. With depressed women, this conflict is often not disclosed for fear of abandonment. Often, this leads to frustration, because conflict is either avoided or the conflict is not resolved. All of these processes created by lack of self-disclosures reinforce the losses experienced in these relationships.

Chapter Seven
Men

The simple answer to the question, why men depress women, is that MOST men are not interested in having a close, confiding relationship. MOST men are not motivated to develop intimacy, nor are they willing to be more self-disclosing. However, MOST men are concerned when, and if, their partner becomes depressed.

So the solution is easy:

(1) Pick one of the few men who do want a close, confiding relationship or
(2) Try to change that non-disclosing distant partner of yours or
(3) Change your attitude about where you look for a close, confiding relationship.

Solution One

There are men who value a close, confiding relationship with a woman but they are in the minority and they tend to work against type of our stereotyped western cultural romantic male figures. These men are reliable, cautious, perhaps a little dull, often introspective and verbal and often viewed by women, prone to depression, as friends, but not lovers. Occasionally, women will choose one of these poor souls, after being discarded by the romantic love of their lives and make these decent, likeable fellows feel like second best all their lives.

The dashing, impulsive, exciting, athletic, adventurous romantic male is NOT interested in a close, confiding relationship. Neither is the ordinary, everyday common man. They are interested in careers, cars, hobbies, etc., and a close relationship for them is a weekend lover, or a woman who will look after them while they pursue their real interests. There is nothing fundamentally wrong with these men—the flaw is in construing them as a possible source of intimacy.

So, if you are a person with anxious attachments, who wants to make a good choice (i.e., for your needs) you should trust who you are attracted toward but don't marry all of them! Have a long courtship, involving honest and deep self-disclosure of values, attitudes and beliefs (especially about relationships) and pick one you like, because you are compatible and dump the others.

Solution Two

If you are already a depressed woman with a distant, non-disclosing relationship but your partner cares about your depression, you might consider marital therapy but be advised this is a risky business. Even presuming the couple who come for therapy are committed, motivated, open and honest and willing to change (and this is asking a lot) the process of therapy will involve a level of self-disclosure, which if it can facilitate intimacy, may also end the relationship. This works two ways. When your man starts to self-disclose those thoughts and feelings you may wish he had kept them to himself! If you were depressed before you knew what was going on inside his head, you may be worse after you hear what he has suppressed so as "not to hurt your feelings."

On the other hand, once you start disclosing the secret fears, shameful thoughts, rigid values, guilty secrets you have been keeping to yourself—he may choose to walk away (your worst fear come true—of if you are a Freudian your secret wish revealed).

However, for most couples a better understanding of their partners' ideas and beliefs, especially about relationships and the marriages they grew up observing, will lead to a closer, confiding relationship.

Solution Three

If we go back to our previous chapters and the concepts of anxious attachments and ambivalent losses, which predispose some, but not all women, to search for a close, confiding relationship with a man, one could say a change of attitude might lead to either acceptance that relationships are seldom what we hope for, or look for closeness in other relationships.

Certainly I have coached many patients over the years (if they have the opportunity) to go back and talk to their parents about their marriage and what they learned from their experiences. The coaching is necessary, so that you approach these significant others not from the point of view of blame or bitterness but as a "naive listener prepared to be amazed." The beliefs we have about relationships are often distortions of the way we construed people earlier in life.

Following recovery from depression, I am amazed how many women find the closeness they have craved in relationships with female friends they had previously ignored, or women they have met during the course of their recovery. The possibility of mutual self-disclosure and compatibility is higher.

Summary

Women are psychologically prone to depression because they are more likely than men to hope their relationship will be a close, confiding match.

Women who experience anxious attachments because of inconsistent bonding experiences with their mothers (who may have been depressed in the post-partem period) are the most at risk because they are not conscious of their mixed feelings regarding close relationships.

Since men construe their relationships from different perspectives, they are often uncomfortable with self-disclosure and closeness is not a goal. This is disappointing to women, who have hoped that they will have a close, confiding relationship and this may trigger and sustain depression.

A new approach to the treatment of depression in women, who attribute their mood disorder to mental discord, would involve facilitating intimacy through the self-disclosure of personal constructs and/or individual therapy, that makes their ambivalence conscious so that their relationship can be construed more realistically and closeness pursued elsewhere.

The Eight Secrets of Close Relationships

Dr. Edward M. Waring and Jennifer A. Waring

This little book is dedicated to the thousands of couples who consented to participate in our marital intimacy research and to the hundreds of couples who have engaged in enhancing marital intimacy therapy.

A Poem

Sticking together
Responding not reacting
To divergent beliefs
Revealing Shadow
Through Self-disclosure
Toward fond sensuality
Tender attachment
Construed harmony

Introduction

The *Eight Secrets of Close Relationships* is a little book designed to encourage you to *reflect* on your relationship, *evaluate* whether you have a close or distant relationship, *assess* your strengths and weaknesses and provide suggestions which you might *choose* if you wish to enhance your marital intimacy.

Chapter one is designed to read and reread like prose poetry in order to provide you with an opportunity to reflect not only on your relationship but the marriage you grew up observing and experiencing. Take a few moments at the end of chapter one to rate your parents' marriage (or the relationship you best remember observing between the ages of five and fifteen) on the eight secrets you have learned (e.g., a 10 would be very affectionate, a 5 would be average and 0 would be a cold relationship). You should be able to make a graph of the relationship that has most influenced your ideas about closeness.

Chapter two provides you with an opportunity to evaluate your relationship and compare your level of closeness with couples in the general population. Chapter three provide descriptions of aspects of the eight secrets.

Chapter four is again designed to provide an opportunity to reflect on the choices you have if you want to have a close, confiding relationship. However, this is not a book of advice or a self-help book—this book is designed to increase your awareness of what a close relationship is—and if you feel you want to enhance your marital intimacy we would suggest reading:

- *Time for Better Marriage* by Don Dinkmeyer and John Carlson, published by American Guidance Service, Circle Pines, Minnesota;
- or *Enhancing Marital Intimacy* by E. M. Waring, published by Routledge, New York, New York; or arrange a referral to a qualified marital counselor.

Chapter One
"Marriages Are Made in Heaven"

A Proverb

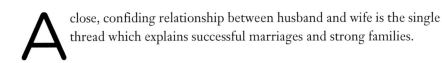 close, confiding relationship between husband and wife is the single thread which explains successful marriages and strong families.

> "The development of intimacy is the major psychosocial
> task of young adulthood"
> (Eric Erickson, 1950).

Fortunate is the child who grows up experiencing and observing parents who like, love and respect each other.

INTIMACY
INTIMACY IS A FEELING OF CLOSENESS
INTIMACY IS A DEPTH OF UNDERSTANDING
INTIMACY IS A GENUINE ACCEPTANCE
INTIMACY THRIVES THROUGH COMMITMENT
INTIMACY GROWS THROUGH SELF-DISCLOSURE

THE EIGHT SECRETS OF CLOSE RELATIONSHIPS

1. CONFLICT RESOLUTION
2. AFFECTION
3. COHESION

4. SEXUALITY
5. IDENTITY
6. COMPATIBILITY
7. AUTONOMY
8. EXPRESSIVENESS

- CONFLICT RESOLUTION
  The couple's capacity for resolving differences of opinion
- AFFECTION
  The couple's expression in word and deed of feelings of warmth, caring and love
- COHESION
  The couple's commitment to the relationship
- SEXUALITY
  The degree to which sexual needs are communicated and fulfilled by the marriage
- IDENTITY
  The couple's level of self-confidence and self-esteem
- COMPATIBILITY
  The couple's sharing of backgrounds, attitudes, activities, and goals
- AUTONOMY
  The success with which the couple gains independence from their families of origin and their offspring
- EXPRESSIVENESS
  The degree to which thoughts, beliefs, attitudes, and feelings are shared within the marriage and as well their level of self-disclosure
- SOCIAL DESIRABILITY
  The extent to which people respond desirably irrespective of the content of the question

Chapter Two
"No Love is Like the First Love"

A Proverb

The Eight Secrets

There are ten statements for each of the eight secrets of intimacy on the following pages. You are to decide which of these statements are true of your marriage and which are false. If you think the statement is TRUE or mostly TRUE of your marriage put "T" for true in front of the statement. If you think that statement is FALSE or mostly FALSE of your marriage, put "F" for false before the statement. When you have answered all ten questions, use the answer key at the bottom of each page to find your total score and mark it on the line provided.

Remember, we would like to know what your marriage seems like to YOU. So DO NOT try to figure out how your spouse will see your marriage, but DO give us your general impression of your marriage for each statement.

As you complete this questionnaire you will notice that some statements are in italics. When you have completed all eight sections of the questionnaire you are ready to find your TOTAL INTIMACY SCORE. Go back to the answer key for each of these italicized statements in order to see if you received a point for your response. Find your TOTAL INTIMACY SCORE by rescoring these forty items. Once you have your score out of 40, subtract your total score on the social desirability scale. This will give you your TOTAL INTIMACY SCORE.

CONFLICT RESOLUTION

- ❏   1.   Differences of opinion never lead to verbal abuse in our relationship
- ❏   2.   Our differences of opinion lead to shouting matches.
- ❏   3.   Discussing problems with my spouse seldom leads to arguments.
- ❏   4.   Old wounds are always reopened when we have differences of opinion.
- ❏   5.   Yelling and screaming play no part in our attempts to re solve our conflict.
- ❏   6.   When there is a difference of opinion, we tend to negotiate a resolution rather than fight.
- ❏   7.   I never hit below the belt when we argue.
- ❏   8.   When we have differences of opinion, my spouse never walks out of the house.
- ❏   9.   During our arguments I never try to depreciate my spouse's point of view.
- ❏ 10.   Sometimes I think all we ever do is argue.

CONFLICT RESOLUTION SCORE:_____

Answer Key

1. T = 1   F = 0
2. T = 0   F = 1
3. T =1   F = 0
4. T = 0   F = 1
5. T = 1   F = 0
6. T = 1   F = 0
7. T= 1   F = 0
8. T= 1   F = 0
9. T = 1   F = 0
10. T = 0   F = 1

AFFECTION

❏	1.	I am at my best when we are together.
❏	2.	I always kiss my spouse goodbye.
❏	3.	I feel that there is a distance between my spouse and me.
❏	4.	Despite being married I often feel lonely.
❏	5.	I often tell my spouse that I love him/her.
❏	6.	We always do something special on our anniversary.
❏	7.	I will never use my love for my spouse as a way to hurt him/her.
❏	8.	I am often unfriendly toward my spouse.
❏	9.	Love is being able to say you're sorry.
❏	10.	Buying gifts shows my affection for my spouse.

AFFECTION SCORE:____

Answer Key

1. T = 1   F = 0
2. T = 1   F = 0
3. T = 0   F = 1
4. T = 0   F = 1
5. T= 1   F = 0
6. T = 1   F = 0
7. T = 1   F = 0
8. T = 0   F = 1
9. T = 1   F = 0
10. T =1   F = 0

COHESION

❏	1.	Without my marriage my life would lack meaning.
❏	2.	Our marital satisfaction is more important than career decisions.
❏	3.	I value our marital relationship above all else.
❏	4.	Even in marriage everyone has to look out for themselves.
❏	5.	When one gets married, it's forever.
❏	6.	In our marriage we try to live by the principle "all for one and one for all."
❏	7.	I am not prepared to put up with my spouse's annoying habits.
❏	8.	I don't really care whether my spouse supports me or not just as long as he/she lets me lead my own life.
❏	9.	I would be willing to compromise my beliefs to make our marriage better.
❏	10.	Most of the time at home I feel like I am just killing time.

COHESION SCORE:____

Answer Key

1. T = 1   F = 0
2. T = 1   F = 0
3. T = 1   F = 0
4. T = 0   F = 1
5. T = 1   F = 0
6. T = 1   F = 0
7. T = 0   F = 1
8. T = 0   F = 1
9. T = 1   F = 0
10. T = 0   F = 1

SEXUALITY

❑   ❑   1.   I ask my spouse for the things that really turn me on.

❑   2.   Sometimes sex seems more like work than play to me.

❑   3.   I think that the importance of sex is highly overrated in marriage.

❑   4.   Sex with my spouse has never been as exciting as in my fantasies.

❑   5.   Our personal closeness is the major determinant of how s atisfactory our sexual relationship is.

❑   6.   Our sexual relationship decreases my frustrations.

❑   7.   My marriage could not possibly be happy without a satis factory sexual life.

❑   8.   I always seem to be in the mood for sex when my spouse is.

❑   9.   My spouse rarely turns away from my sexual advances.

❑   10.   Our sexual relationship influences our level of closeness.

SEXUALITY SCORE:___

Answer Key

1.   T = 1   F = 0
2.   T = 0   F = 1
3.   T = 0   F = 1
4.   T = 0   F = 1
5.   T = 1   F=0
6.   T = 1   F = 0
7.   T = 1   F = 0
8.   T = 1   F = 0
9.   T = 1   F = 0
10. T = 1   F = 0

IDENTITY

❏   1.   I often feel insecure in social situations.
❏   2.   Compared to other people that I know I lack self-esteem.
❏   3.   I have a strong sense of who I am.
❏   4.   I really don't think that I am very good at most things.
❏   5.   I feel that I am the person I would like to be.
❏   6.   I am embarrassed when I am the center of attention.
❏   7.   When I compare myself to most other people, I like myself.
❏   8.   I am sometimes afraid that people will see a part of me that I am not aware of.
❏   9.   There are many aspects of my personality that I do not like.
❏   10.   Other people usually have more to offer in a conversation than I do.

IDENTITY SCORE:___

Answer Key

1.   T = 0   F = 1
2.   T = 0   F = 1
3.   T = 1   F = 0
4.   T = 0   F = 1
5.   T = 1   F = 0
6.   T = 0   F = 1
7.   T = 1   F = 0
8.   T = 0   F = 1
9.   T = 0   F = 1
10. T = 0   F = 1

COMPATIBILITY

❏	1.	I wish my spouse enjoyed more the activities that I enjoy.
❏	2.	We seem to work out how to share the chores at our house.
❏	3.	My spouse and I share the same philosophy of life.
❏	4.	My spouse frequently helps when I am doing an unpleasant chore.
❏	5.	My spouse and I share the same goals in life.
❏	6.	My spouse and I like to do things for self-improvement together.
❏	7.	My spouse and I have worked out the male-female house hold roles to both our satisfactions.
❏	8.	My spouse did not try to make me change after we got married.
❏	9.	I found it difficult to make changes in my lifestyle after we were married.
❏	10.	My spouse's sociability adds a positive aspect to our relationship.

COMPATIBILITY SCORE:____

Answer Key

1. T = 0   F = 1
2. T = 1   F = 0
3. T = 1   F = 0
4. T = 1   F = 0
5. T = 1   F = 0
6. T = 1   F = 0
7. T = 1   F = 0
8. T = 1   F = 0
9. T = 0   F = 1
10. T= 1   F = 0

AUTONOMY

❑   1.   I enjoy spending time with my in-laws.

❑   2.   Whenever we visit my spouse's parents, I feel awkward be cause I have nothing to talk about.

❑   3.   My in-laws' advice is often appreciated and welcome.

❑   4.   When all the relatives get together, I feel awkward and un comfortable.

❑   5.   We are lucky to have relatives to whom we can go for help.

❑   6.   It is a real effort for me to try and get along with my spouse's parents.

❑   7.   I feel that my parents interfere in our relationship.

❑   8.   Family reunions are one highlight of our social life.

❑   9.   Our children interfere with the time we have together.

❑   10.   Our marriage would be better if our parents didn't meddle in our problems.

AUTONOMY SCORE:___

Answer Key

1.   T = 1   F = 0
2.   T = 0   F = 1
3.   T = 1   F = 0
4.   T = 0   F = 1
5.   T = 1   F = 0
6.   T = 0   F = 1
7.   T = 0   F = 1
8.   T = 1   F = 0
9.   T = 0   F = 1
10. T = 0   F = 1

EXPRESSIVENESS

❏   1.   If there is one thing that my spouse and I are good at, it's talking about our feelings to each other.

❏   2.   Often I only pretend to listen when my spouse talks.

❏   3.   I prefer to keep my personal thoughts to myself.

❏   4.   I enjoy sharing my feelings with my spouse.

❏   5.   I always try to give my spouse my full attention when he/she is talking to me.

❏   6.   I often read the newspaper or watch TV when my spouse is trying to talk to me.

❏   7.   I would lie to my spouse if I thought it would keep the peace.

❏   8.   My personal secrets would hurt my spouse.

❏   9.   I can say anything I want to my spouse.

❏ 10.   I always take time to listen to my spouse.

EXPRESSIVENESS SCORE:___

Answer Key

1. T = 1   F = 0
2. T = 0   F = 1
3. T = 0   F= 1
4. T = 1   F = 0
5. T = 1   F = 0
6. T = 0   F= 1
7. T = 0   F = 1
8. T = 0   F = 1
9. T = 1   F = 0
10. T = 1   F = 0

SOCIAL DESIRABILITY

- ❏ 1. I don't think any couple lives together with greater harmony than my mate and me.
- ❏ 2. I have some needs that are not being met by my marriage.
- ❏ 3. My mate has all of the qualities I have always wanted in a mate.
- ❏ 4. My marriage is not a perfect success.
- ❏ 5. My marriage could be happier than it is.
- ❏ 6. I have never regretted my marriage not even for a moment.
- ❏ 7. I don't think that anyone could possibly he happier than my mate and I when we are with one another.
- ❏ 8. There are times when I do not feel a great deal of love and affection for my mate.
- ❏ 9. There are some things about my mate that I do not like.
- ❏ 10. Every new thing I have learned about my mate has pleased me.

SOCIAL DESIRABILITY SCORE:___

Answer Key

1. T = 1   F = 0
2. T = 0   F = 1
3. T = 1   F = 0
4. T = 0   F = 1
5. T = 0   F= 1
6. T = 1   F = 0
7. T = 1   F = 0
8. T = 0   F = 1
9. T = 0   F = 1
10. T = 1   F = 0

TOTAL INTIMACY SCORE

Add up your answers from the first 5 questions on each scale.

TOTAL SCORE:_____

Subtract your score on social desirability.

SOCIAL DESIRABILITY SCORE:_____

TOTAL — SOCIAL DESIRABILITY = TOTAL INTIMACY

SCORE:____

Chapter Three
What Your Answers
Reveal About Your Relationship

N ow that you have completed the questionnaire, you are likely wondering what your answers can tell you about your relationship. On the following pages, descriptions are provided for your score on each facet of intimacy. On average, couples in the general population score between 6 and 8 for each sub-test. If you score higher than this on a particular measure of intimacy then keep up the good work! You are doing very well in comparison to most couples and you can continue to build on your strengths. If you score below 6, on a particular measure, this indicates that this is an area of challenge for your relationship. Don't despair. This does not mean that your relationship can not be enhanced. In chapter four, suggestions are provided for making improvements in order to achieve the satisfying marriage that you desire.

CONFLICT RESOLUTION
What your score reveals:

0   Differences of opinion are frequent and volatile. Sometimes it seems like all you ever do is argue. Arguments usually lead to yelling and screaming matches filled with insults and verbal abuse. This relationship is characterized by verbal warfare.

1   Arguments are frequent and intense and spiral into yelling and screaming as verbal arsenals. The same issues arise repeatedly and are never resolved. Each repetition of the same old issue gets more intense and ugly. No thought is given to rational discussion but the matter of importance is establishing "who is right."

2   When arguments occur they are intense, painful and disrespectful. Instead of trying to pinpoint the real conflict and come to a mutually satisfying decision, you yell, scream, insult, retaliate and do whatever it takes to get your point across. Such persistent arguments lead to feelings of resentment, which can slowly erode the relationship.

3   Differences of opinion sometimes lead to verbal abuse. The goal of arguments in such a marriage are to hurt, retaliate and above all else, to be right. Such beliefs rarely lead to rational problem solving because the more you fight the greater the hostility, distance and resent in the marriage.

4   Some differences of opinion can be solved rationally, while others end in shouting matches. You often try to negotiate a resolution but when emotions are running high insults begin to fly. You find it difficult to see your spouse's point of view and at times feel attacked during disagreements.

5   Overall your relationship is tension free. Certain topics lead to arguments that seem to go on unresolved, while other difficulties are handled with negotiation and respect for the other's point of view.

6   You are a good problem solver. Yelling and shouting is not the way that differences of opinion are generally resolved in your relationship. Keeping harmony in your relationship is more important than having

the last say, or being right. Although you do not always agree with your spouse, you are receptive to other points of view.

7   Discussing problems with your partner seldom leads to arguments. The ease with which you handle conflict is a source of strength in your marriage. You are respectful of your partner point of view and care about solving problems amicably. You rarely play on your partner's vulnerabilities during arguments by intentionally opening old wounds.

8   When conflicts arise you show mutual respect for each other's opinions. Openly discussing your problems allows you to live in a relaxed environment where you are not afraid to let you opinion be known. You mutually participate in decisions and reach mutually satisfying solutions.

9   When differences of opinion arise they are discussed calmly, rationally and in a manner that shows mutual respect. The relationship is your priority so you do not feel like you need to intimidate in order to get your point across.

10   While differences of opinion occur in all marriages, the way they are handled varies from marriage to marriage. When differences occur you show mutual respect for each other's opinion and are able to pinpoint the real issue. You are able to seek and focus on areas of agreement and mutually participate in decisions. Your relationship is characterized by peace and harmony.

AFFECTION
What your score reveals:

0   Your relationship sorely lacks affection. You do not greet each other with kisses nor verbally express your love for one another. You are often unfriendly toward your spouse, use words to hurt and have a hard time saying sorry when you know that you are in the wrong. Such an absence of expressions of love and caring leads to feelings of distance and loneliness. You often feel like your relationship detracts from your life rather than enhancing it.

1   You often feel unloved in your marriage. Your lack of verbal, emotional and physical expressions of affection leads you to feel lonely in your marriage. When you are together you often feel as though your spouse does not get you at your best.

2   You do not have the love in a marriage that leads to feelings of closeness, unity and togetherness. As a result there is often distance and loneliness in your relationship.

3   Sometimes you find that it is easier to be nice to friends, neighbors and coworkers than it is to be friendly to your spouse. Without the intimacy of affection in your marriage, you may feel as though you are drifting apart.

4   The love you once felt for your partner seems to have waned. You no longer take the time to verbally express your love for one another. While there are some expressions of affection in your marriage, you miss the times when you showered each other with kindness.

5   You and your spouse may love each other but at times you forget the importance of sharing this love. When you take your love for granted by assuming love without sharing it, you may feel as though you are not as close as you used to be because you do not share as many expressions of love.

6   You love your spouse but at times you forget the importance of showing it. You generally express your feelings to your partner and try not to use your love to hurt your partner when you are feeling vulnerable.

7   You and your spouse are quite affectionate. While you sometimes for-
     get that sharing your love is important, overall you feel a great sense
     of companionship and togetherness in your relationship.

8   Your shared affection is a definite strength in your marriage. You show
     kindness and warmth each day and take time to celebrate your love
     on special occasions. Your partner enhances your life and you feel at
     your best when you are together.

9   You and your spouse share your love verbally, emotionally and phys-
     ically. You feel that your marriage is special and take the time to re-
     mind each other of your feelings. You take extra care to be loving
     toward your spouse and are careful not to use your love to inflict pain.

10   Your relationship brings out the best in you. You are openly affection-
     ate and take the time to express your love verbally and physically. You
     celebrate your love on special occasions and through kindness toward
     each other every day. You are able to say sorry as you would rather be
     happy than right. You do not use your spouse's disclosures to you as
     weapons during disagreements.

COHESION
What your score reveals:

0   You are not willing to make many sacrifices for your marriage. Your life, desires and dreams come first and all else is second. Love does not always last forever and, therefore, you need to look out for yourself. You are satisfied with your relationship as long as it does not involve too much compromise.

1   Even though you are married, you function very independently. You believe that you have to look out for yourself in life. Marriages come and go but life must go on. You find it very difficult to compromise. You are happy as long as you can live your own life and do you own thing.

2   You have difficulty trusting that relationships can last and as a result you make sure to take care of yourself and your own needs. Independence is very important to you and it is necessary for you to have your own separate life apart from your marriage. You do not feel like you need to check in with your mate on all matters.

3   You find it difficult to compromise when important decisions are being made. You like to make your own plans and decisions. While you want a lasting relationship, you sometimes fear that most relationships do not last. You are not willing to compromise too much of yourself in order to make your marriage work.

4   You struggle with your partner over issues such as how much time to spend together, how much independence or dependence each partner should have and what are your short-term and long-term plans. You enjoy making independent decisions and taking care of your own needs.

5   You feel as though you have a healthy balance between independence and dependence in your relationship. Your relationship is important to you but no such much that you are willing to compromise your identity.

6   Your relationship is special and you value each other's contributions. Your relationship gives your life meaning and mutual satisfaction is essential to your happiness.

7   You feel as though your marriage is going to last forever. Your relationship enhances your life and is valued above all else. You rely on each other for support and value each other's opinions.

8   You and your spouse function well as a cohesive unit. Mutual decisions are made regarding important issues and your mutual satisfaction takes precedence over all else. You look out for each other and look forward to a long, lasting marriage.

9   Your spouse's support is important to you. While you maintain your own identity, you function as a unit and make important decisions together. Your marriage is the most important relationship in your life and you make sure to love, cherish and support one another.

10   When you got married you planned it to be forever. You and your spouse look out for each other and always put your relationship above all else. Without your marriage your life would lack meaning. Your marriage enhances your life and you support each other's endeavors,

SEXUALITY
What your score reveals:

0   Your sex life is a source of frustration and disappointment. You do not share your sexual fantasies with your partner and your sex life lacks excitement. You feel that sex is overrated and is more effort than fun. You do not use sexual activities to decrease your frustrations as you do not find sex with your partner very fulfilling.

1   You think that sex is overrated in marriage. Your sexuality is not a determinant of closeness in your relationship and sex seems more like work than play. You do not share your fantasies and turn-ons and so your spouse does not know what to do to excite you.

2   You are not satisfied with your sex life. You lack open communication about sexual matters and as a result your partner does not know what makes you happy in bed. Sex is often a source of frustration and leaves you feeling unfulfilled and distant from your partner.

3   Your sexual relationship is lacking in excitement and fulfillment. You both seem to be in the mood for sex at different times. You are hesitant or embarrassed to share your sexual preferences and turn-ons with your partner and as a result you are not getting what you want from your sexual relationship.

4   You feel that your sexual relationship could definitely improve. At times your sexual relationship is fulfilling and at others sex seems like work rather than play. You feel that sex is important in marriage but it is not the major determinant of how close you feel to your partner.

5   Like most marriages, your sexual relationship waxes and wanes over time. Overall, you are satisfied with your sexual relationship but would like to add some excitement. Your sex life generally decreases your frustrations and brings you and your partner closer together.

6   You feel satisfied with your sex life but are open to improvement. You and your partner share your turn-ons with each other and your sex life is a large component of your feelings of closeness with your spouse. You generally share a similar sex drive with your partner although there are times when you are not in the mood.

7 You and your partner share a satisfying sexual relationship. Like every marriage, there are times when you are not in the mood for sex but overall you ask your spouse for what turns you on and are genuinely interested in what excites your partner.

8 You and your partner have a sexual relationship that enhances your marriage. You have similar sex drives and attitudes regarding the importance of sex. Your sexuality decreases frustrations and promotes unity in the relationship.

9 You have an exciting sex life that decreases daily frustrations and increases feelings of intimacy and closeness. You know what makes each other excited and share your fantasies with each other. Sex is important to your relationship and you take the time to share your sexuality.

10 You and your partner have an exciting and fulfilling sexual relationship. You are open about your turn-ons and sexual fantasies and your sexuality enhances your feelings of closeness and intimacy.

IDENTITY
What your score reveals:

0   You lack self-esteem and do not like to be the center of attention. When you compare yourself to others you feel that you always come up short. There are many things about yourself that you do not like. All these negative feelings can lead to the belief that you are never good enough.

1   You are very hard on yourself and do not recognize your assets. You lack self-esteem and do not have a strong sense of who you are. Because you feel that you do not measure up to others, you keep your thoughts to yourself in most social situations. It is hard to allow yourself to be loved by others when you do not love yourself.

2   You feel insecure about your abilities and tend to be an observer of life rather than a participant. This can lead you to feel disconnected from your partner. You generally keep your feelings and opinions to yourself in social situations. You have a fear of being rejected.

3   You are your own worst critic. Feeling insecure and failing to acknowledge your strengths makes it very difficult to achieve happiness. You have a great deal of difficulty accepting compliments because you generally do not believe them. You feel that you are not the person you desire to be but you are not sure how to change so that you feel better about yourself.

4   Your self-esteem is somewhat low but you also have some strengths that make you feel worthwhile. While you feel that you often do not measure up when you compare yourself with others, you generally have a sense of who you are.

5   You have average self-esteem in comparison to the general population. While you can be hard on yourself at times, you realize that you do have much to offer to others. You may hang back in social situations with strangers but feel comfortable to be yourself when with friends.

6   You have a sense of who you are and what makes you happy. While there may be aspects of your personality that you do not particularly like, you are forgiving of those qualities. You may feel that other peo-

ple seem more confident than you do but at the same time, you recognize that you have much to offer.

7   You have good self-esteem, self-confidence and self-acceptance. Everyone has their days when they are feeling down but your strong sense of identity guides you through your decisions and goals. You like who you are and recognize your assets.

8   Your strong sense of identity is a source of inner strength. When things are not going as well as you would like, your confidence leads you to solutions. You focus on your strengths and are not generally intimated in social situations.

9   You have a healthy dose of self-confidence and self-esteem. You know who you are and what you want out of life. You recognize your areas of strength and celebrate them without getting too concerned about areas of weakness.

10 You have a strong sense of identity, confidence and self-esteem. When you compare yourself to others, you like what you see in yourself. You feel that you have many strengths and have a great deal to offer to others. Social situations do not intimidate you but rather provide opportunities to thrive by sharing your ideas with others. Knowing yourself helps you to know what you want out of your marriage.

COMPATIBILITY
What your score reveals:

0   You have precious little in common with your spouse. You have different philosophies on life and dissimilar goals. You do not have unconditional love but rather a relationship in which you and your partner try and change one another. Such a relationship can lead to power struggles and feelings of frustration and loneliness since you do not feel free to be yourself.

1   At the present time, you and your partner have many incompatibilities in your relationship. You differ in terms of philosophies, goals, role expectations, responsibilities and activities. Such discrepancies can lead to a lack of understanding and acceptance of one another.

2   You and your partner do not have very much in common. While you may see a few things in a similar light, overall you are very aware of your differences. Having few shared interests can lead to a lack of togetherness in your marriage.

3   You do not share many interests with your partner. While your overall goals may be similar, you differ in terms of many day-to-day issues regarding how to spend your spare time and how to divide roles within the relationship.

4   Shared interests, values and goals are something that you need to work on with your partner. There may be areas of similarity but differences are emphasized which lead to a lack of shared activities.

5   You share many philosophies, goals and interests in your relationship but there are also areas of incompatibility that need to be addressed.

6   You and your partner have much in common. By continuing to focus on the similarities and strengths in your marriage your friendship and feelings of companionship will continue to grow.

7   Your compatibility is a source of strength in your marriage. While there are differences, your similarities in terms of goals and values guide your marriage and provide a sense of togetherness.

8   You and your partner are very compatible. While you may not see eye to eye on every single matter, you are similar in ways that are the most important. You share common philosophies, goals and outlooks on life that allow you to be yourself and pursue your interests while respecting the interests of your partner.

9   Your high compatibility is a source of strength in your marriage. You share the same philosophy of life, values and expectations. You love your mate for who they are and this unconditional love is reciprocated. Your common goals are a unifying force that leads you to pursue similar activities and goals.

10 You and your partner are highly compatible. In such a marriage, your partner is generally your best friend, which leads to feelings of belonging and closeness. Your love for each other is unconditional and you respect each other's differences and unique qualities that add to the relationship.

AUTONOMY
What your score reveals:

0   You see your in-laws as a constant source of stress. You feel unaccepted and uncomfortable around your spouse's family and you feel that your in-laws interfere in your life. You are facing the world alone with little family support. As a couple you lack friends.

1   In-laws provide a nearly universal and potentially dangerous threat to marital happiness. You perceive your in-laws as interfering and critical. Some parents have a hard time letting go and you question whether your spouse is married to you or his family. Friends or children may be a focus of distress.

2   You and your in-laws rarely see eye to eye which leads to tension in your marital relationship. Few partners can criticize their in-laws without risking criticism of their own parents in return. Disagreements over issues relating to your in-laws pull you in different directions. Friends and children do not enhance your relationship.

3   It is difficult to be in a relationship in which you have to make a choice regarding your loyalty. When in-laws give unsolicited advice you and your partner try to defend your parents and their motives. This causes unnecessary stress, as we did not pick our relatives and cannot answer for their behavior but only for our own. You have some friends but children may be a burden.

4   Overall, your in-laws do not cause much friction in your relationship but sometimes you wish they would butt out, live their own lives and mind their own business. You sometimes feel awkward and uncomfortable around your in-laws. However, they generally keep their distance and sometimes offer encouragement and support. There is some pleasure from friends and children.

5   You have a healthy balance between making your spouse your priority while balancing the needs of relatives and in-laws. At times you feel frustrated when in-laws offer advice that was not requested but overall, your spouse's family as well as your own adds an element of security in an insecure world. Too much attention may be focused on friends and/or children.

6   You function well as a couple independently and with friends and relatives. You are generally able to handle differences of opinion regarding in-laws by making the relationship your priority. You feel lucky to have relatives that you can rely on in times of need. Friends and children are an asset to your relationship.

7   You enjoy spending time with your in-laws and have a lot to add to their discussions. You feel accepted for who you are which makes you at ease in your relationships with friends, relatives and in-laws. Your parents and your in-laws respect your privacy and leave you alone to make important decisions but are available when you request their advice. Your children enhance your marriage.

8   Although parents should always be important to us, they cannot be the first priority in a healthy marriage. It is the responsibility of the spouse to set limits on parental involvement. You come first in your marriage and have a healthy relationship with your in-laws in which they add support and encouragement. Friends and children are enjoyed.

9   Your needs take precedence over the needs of your spouse's in-laws and this maintains your marital harmony. You genuinely care about your relatives and enjoy spending time with them, friends and children.

10   Relatives add a supportive and welcome influence in your life. Their advice is generally helpful and non-interfering and you feel comfortable and at ease around them. You know that they will be there for you in times of difficulty and you cherish their involvement in your relationship. Friends and children are a joy.

EXPRESSIVENESS
What your score reveals:

0   Positive forms of communication are lacking in your relationship. You neither communicate with nor listen to each other and may be keeping harmful secrets that could destroy your marriage. You are in a relationship in which you and your partner are virtual strangers.

1   You keep your thoughts, feelings and desires to yourself and are often not receptive to your partner's feelings. This can lead to feelings of isolation, distance and a lack of belonging in the relationship.

2   For the most part you keep thoughts, feelings and desires to yourself and lack the time, energy and interest to listen to your spouse.

3   You keep your private world to yourself and may feel threatened by the idea of revealing too much of yourself. You may find that you can pay attention to your spouse on occasion when they are sharing information that is interesting to you. However, for the most part, there is disinterest when listening to your spouse.

4   You do not easily reveal your feelings but are able to talk about ideas and facts. You may try to listen to your spouse but find that you are easily distracted and often not interested in what they have to say.

5   Some ideas, desires, opinions and feelings are openly expressed while others are not. Revelations that may be hurtful are sometimes kept secret which can lead to some feelings of distance in the marriage. While you generally listen to your spouse, there are times that you find it difficult to give your full attention.

6   Overall, your relationship is characterized by good communication skills. You try your best to share your thoughts and feelings with your partner and to be a supportive listener.

7   You have effective communication skills, which enable you to feel close to and understood by your partner.

8   You generally share your feelings in an open, caring way and communicate negative thoughts in a respectful manner. You are able to affirm positive feelings by expressing ways you accept and value each other.

9   You and your partner really listen to each other and share your feelings, even though by sharing feelings you risk rejection. By giving and receiving feedback without demanding change you demonstrate that you care about each other and your relationship.

10 You have excellent communication in your relationship. Desires, feelings and opinions are shared. This allows you to be open, flexible, honest and genuine. Your expressiveness frees you to be yourself and nourishes the marriage.

TOTAL INTIMACY SCORE
What your score reveals:

Optimal Intimacy (30-40)

One in every ten couples who marry will develop optimal intimacy. People in such relationships generally come from families who share open communication and intimacy. You have had close relationships with parents, siblings and peers. You know who you are, what you want and whom you want to be with. You and your spouse have a good sense of humor in dealing with life's ups and downs. You and your partner share similar values, goals and attitudes. As a result, you rarely have differences of opinion. You verbally express respect, caring, loving and liking for each other. You are committed to your marriage, which is your most important relationship. You are actively involved with family, friends and community. You communicate openly, honestly and respectfully and share your inner most thoughts with each other. People with such high levels of intimacy tend to share remarkable physical and emotional health.

Adequate Intimacy (20-30)

Two out of every ten couples develop adequate marital intimacy. This type of intimacy involves areas of strength and areas of weakness in the relationship but weaknesses such as lack of compatibility or difficulties with sexuality are perceived accurately and acknowledged. You feel that your strengths generally outweigh your weaknesses. You try your best to accept and adjust to your difficulties.

Pseudo-Intimacy (10-20)

Two out of every ten couples develop pseudo-intimacy. Your areas of weakness outweigh the strengths in your relationship but for a variety of reasons you stay together. You hunger for intimate love and have decided to settle for marital satisfaction and a sense of family. You feel that your relationship lacks affection and compatibility and that you are lacking a close, confiding relationship with your partner.

Deficient Intimacy (<10)

Two out of every ten couples who marry stay together despite a lack of overt closeness. The average couple in society is between pseudo-intimacy and deficient intimacy, a far cry from our cultural myths regarding marriage. Marriages with deficient intimacy are characterized by conflict, physical abuse, alcoholism, affairs, chronic grudges, alliances with children and chaotic family life. Although you lack affection, have poor communication, frequent arguments and poor sexuality, you feel committed to the relationship and may experience moments of joy.

Divorce, Separation, Abandonment, etc.

Three of out of every ten couples will divorce or separate for a variety of reasons without developing closeness. Without awareness of one's contributions to the marital discord future relationships will also be distorted.

Chapter Four
Eight Golden Rules of Close Relationships

1. NEVER ARGUE WITH YOUR PARTNER.
2. SHOWER YOUR PARTNER WITH AFFECTION.
3. YOUR MARRIAGE IS YOUR MOST IMPORTANT RELA-TIONSHIP.
4. FACILITATE YOUR PARTNER'S SENSUAL ROMATIC PLEASURE.
5. KNOW YOURSELF THROUGH YOUR PARTNER'S EYES.
6. CHOSE TO BE INVOLVED IN YOUR PARTNER'S INTER-ESTS.
7. CHERISH YOUR FAMILY AND FRIENDS.
8. SELF-DISCLOSE YOUR PERSONAL CONSTRUCTS.

1. NEVER ARGUE WITH YOUR PARTNER.
   a) Everyone feels angry sometimes.
   b) Partners choose how to experience and express anger.
   c) Fighting always produces distance, not closeness.
   d) Respect your partner's differences of opinion.
   e) Respond rather than react to how your partner construes issues.
   f) Problems are opportunities to be solved.
   g) Resolving conflict produces closeness.
   h) Problem solving feels good.
   i) Never Argue with Your Partner.

CONFLICT RESOLUTION
Couples who fight don't believe me when I tell them that four out of ten cou-

ples never argue! One group who never fight is so compatible that they have nothing to fight about. A second group who never fights is afraid of the consequences. Unfortunately, those who fight and those who don't fight don't like to spend time together. Thus, the rationalization that all couples fight is easy to maintain. The problem is that construing fighting as normal means you aren't motivated to change. The truth is that all arguing, fighting and abuse leads to distance not closeness.

The same is true of anger. People say anger is a normal feeling—everybody gets angry. The truth is that each of us experiences more or less anger and choose to express anger in different ways. Expressing anger at your spouse leads to distance—accepting that you are a person prone to anger allows you a choice. If you have the courage to give up denial and rationalization you can choose to NEVER fight or express anger at your spouse again.

Those of you who are prone to experiencing and expressing anger at your spouse will be

thinking…that's impossible! You will be right if you don't choose to change your attitude toward fighting and anger.

If you accept the premise that everyone construes relationships differently than conflict—difference of opinion—becomes an opportunity to learn more about others—including your spouse—and become more flexible rather than trying to make the world conform to your point of view.

Some people would rather be RIGHT than be CLOSE. You can choose to RESPOND when angry rather than REACT. Responding involves encouragement of your spouse to disclose their explanation of why they construe an issue in a different light. This allows opportunities for greater understanding and for possible alternative solutions to conflicts. Conflict resolution depends on attitudes of respect for one's spouse's views, flexibility in considering multiple viewpoints and the courage to try alternate solutions rather than engaging in another repetitive and hurtful argument.

2. SHOWER YOUR PARTNER WITH AFFECTION.

a)   Express your love every day.

b)   Choose to show affection.

c)   Encourage your partner's growth.

d)   Kind words

e)   Gentle touches

f)   Warm hugs

g)   Support your partner's mixture of frailties.

h)   Polite and tactful

AFFECTION

When asked, "Who are you most polite toward?" people name their boss, their coworkers, strangers, etc. NOT their spouse! "Home is where you let you hair down" is a relationship myth. We all KNOW how much we appreciate a kind word, appreciation, gratefulness expressed BUT we don't CHOOSE to say and do these expressions of affection to our spouse. Why?

Most couples with discord tell me they don't express affection because they don't feel affectionate! They explain that it would not feel GENUINE to express affection when they are feeling dislike or disgust. So I ask, "Do you feel that way all the time?" If they do feel negative all the time…they are describing an attitude…feelings tend to come and go. You have a choice to change your attitude and express affection between bad feelings. Surprisingly, the more people express affection the more likely they are to feel affection!

Expressing affection—liking, caring and respect—can be done through deeds and not just words. Thoughtful messages, considerate words, spontaneous gifts, hugs and kisses are only a few of the many ways to express affection. AND, people who receive affectionate words and deeds are most likely to return the favor.

So what's stopping you? A bad attitude? Remember, improving your marriage begins with you (after all, you are the one who is reading this little book). People who have never experienced affection often cop out by saying they don't know how—or maybe you are one of those selfish or self-preoccupied creatures we hear so much about these days?

Only one problem! How is your spouse going to react to this new, positive and affectionate you? They will be surprised. They may think you are up to something. Tell them you are—you are after a close, confiding relationship.

3. YOUR MARRIAGE IS YOUR MOST IMPORTANT RELATIONSHIP.
a) Time for a better marriage
b) Trust your partner.
c) Work toward closeness.
d) Marriage is a commitment.
e) Your partner comes first.
f) Your family comes second.
g) Your work comes third.
h) Don't sweat the small stuff.

COHESION

The definition of cohesion is "a sticking together" or "tendency to hold to-gether" or in physics "an attraction between molecules of the same kind...." Not a bad metaphor! Cohesion is about commitment, persistence and being held together by the energy created when you decide your marriage is the most important relationship in your life—yes, that's right, more important than your career, your family, your children, your hobby.

So this is the big one—the deal breaker the crux of the matter! If you are not passionate about your marriage the result, as they say, is a waste of time. If you choose to put the same energy, curiosity, drive, passion into developing a close, confiding relationship as you do into...you have a chance. You can fill in the blank.

Cohesion is NOT being resigned to staying in a miserable marriage. Cohesion is being committed to making time for a better marriage! I am always surprised by couples who are proud of staying together for thirty or forty or fifty miserable years. I think it is a shame that they have exposed friends and family to a lifeless charade.

However, it does take COURAGE to admit and accept responsibility for a distant relationship. Not only do you have to turn failure into a challenging opportunity but you have to have the GUTS to give up marriages most con-venient rationalization—"I would be perfectly happy if I wasn't married to that turkey."

Cohesion is accepting that you picked a turkey in the first place or you have contributed to making an ugly duckling out of a swan. Cohesion is putting your heart and soul into changing your attitudes, beliefs and behavior and committing yourself to the consequences. A close, confiding relationship pro-vides couples with the strength to overcome life's hassles and the peace of mind to fully enjoy life's pleasures.

4. FACILITATE YOUR PARTNER'S SENSUAL ROMANTIC PLEASURE.
a) Romance comes first.
b) Affection is second.
c) Share your fantasies.
d) Disclose your preferences.
e) Have fun.
f) Focus on pleasure, not performance.
g) Explore mutual turn-ons.
h) Read The Joy of Sex.

SEXUALITY.
Isn't it amazing how often marriage ruins a robust, sensual and sexual relationship? In our age of so-called sexual openness and enlightenment most couples are sexually active before marriage. When I ask about the couple's sexuality on the honeymoon—"Oh, Dr. Waring, you are so old fashioned—we have been sexually active for years—but—now that you mention the honeymoon, things didn't go so well."

Why not? Because sexuality is associated with romance, adventure, freedom and too many couples forget that with marriage conventionality, duty and responsibility dampen ardor. So, unless both partners continue to make time for romance and adventure, their sensual enjoyment will decrease. The above is especially true if the couple has infants or adolescent children.

Even more surprising is the lack of awareness amongst couples that violence, arguments and open expression of anger guarantees a decrease in sexuality. Nobody wants to make love to a spouse who has hurt them, insulted them or they are frightened of their temper.

Generally, the closer the relationship the more enjoyable the sexuality although the pattern of the sexuality may vary considerably. There is, however, one exception. Some couples who are quite devoted and loving come from backgrounds of prudishness and inhibition at one extreme or abuse at the other extreme. These couples often benefit from education (like Alex Comfort's book, The Joy of Sex) or from specific counseling. Specific sexual dysfunctions should be addressed early in a marriage because they can be the cause of distancing.

The MORAL of this story is that closeness is usually associated with robust sensual, sexual pleasure and joyful sex contributes to intimacy.

5. KNOW YOURSELF THROUGH YOUR PARTNER'S EYES.
a) Who you are
b) What you want
c) Who you want to be with
d) What you want to do
e) Shared
f) Reflected
g) Integrated
h) Defines us

IDENTITY

One assumes that knowing who we are, what we want to do and who we want to be with is a psychosocial challenge we have successfully resolved in adolescence. Supposedly during courtship we can choose to reveal our important beliefs, values and attitudes and we are comfortable with our traits of personality, character and habits. Sadly, many people lack self-esteem and self-respect and are either confused about their own identify or develop a NEGATIVE identity in opposition to people they respect.

THE PROBLEM for dating and courtship is that many people will present a PERSONA that is not genuine and is designed to court acceptance through concealment. Often this results in conflict after marriage when one's true values or suppressed attitudes emerge. One or the other spouse may feel resentful that they have been deceived. The couple may feel ashamed due to not measuring up to expectations.

PARADOXICALLY, marriage provides a rare opportunity to explore one's identity through honest self-disclosure. If one has the courage to make statements starting with "I am…I believe…I need…I feel…," one has the opportunity to reflect on feedback given by a spouse who knows you regarding the accuracy of your self-assessments. This takes courage to risk exposure and this takes trust that your partner's feedback will be both honest and constructive.

ODDLY, one of the great motivators to chance comes from the discomfort that others see us differently from how we see ourselves. If we are able and willing to see our mixture of frailties through our spouse's eyes, we have the opportunity to become the ideal self we imagine. Self-esteem and self-respect GROW through honest self-appraisal and not through superficial and shallow reassurance and support.

6. CHOOSE TO BE INVOLVED IN YOUR PARTNER'S INTERESTS.

a) Interests
b) Values
c) Attitudes
d) Style
e) Similarities
f) Produce Liking
g) Loving
h) Respect

COMPATABILITY

One of the great secrets of close relationships is that LIKING may be more important in the long run than LOVING. One of the great rules of psychology is that we like people who are similar to ourselves. Similarity of beliefs, values, attitudes, personality, style and even appearance all contribute to compatibility. Couples who are highly compatible have the luxury of not needing conflict resolution skills because there is no conflict. So choosing a spouse due to similarities is a sure way to develop liking, loving and a close relationship.

BUT, what about all the poor souls who are already married and incompatible? TIME for an ATTITUDE TRANSPLANT. Forget whining about different interests. Forget trying to change your spouse's beliefs. TIME for you to develop an interest in your spouse! You have forgotten that you were once fascinated by your spouse (that's what falling in love is all about!). JOIN your spouse at the OPERA or the WWF. Be flexible and have FUN in spite of yourself. DISCOVER where your spouse's beliefs, attitudes and values came from.

We are amazed how often spouses will focus on lack of compatibility as a roadblock to close relationship. It would seem more important for them to be RIGHT in the way they construe their spouse's traits or attitudes than be FLEXIBLE and be happy. For example, if you construe your spouse as inconsiderate (or selfish, or lazy…) ask YOURSELF how you managed to pick an inconsiderate person out of all the people to choose. If you react, "They weren't that way when I met them," our response is, "What have you done to them!"

The ONLY way to increase compatibility in a relationship is to CHANGE yourself— change your attitude and construe your partner in a new and challenging light. SOMETIMES differences can be accepted and enjoyed.

7. CHERISH YOUR FAMILY AND FRIENDS.
a) A couple relates
b) To parents
c) Siblings
d) Children
e) Friends
f) Acquaintances
g) In a Positive
h) Accepting Manner

AUTONOMY

Every couple needs to define and develop their relationship to parents, family, children, friends and the communities they live in.

Close relationships are defined by couples who have positive interactions with friends and families while not allowing people to intrude. So don't let your mother-in-law set your agenda! Don't let your children become the only focus of your relationship! Don't let your friends try to convince you that you need to behave in certain ways!

Autonomy starts with going steady, getting engaged and with the wedding. Each step in this process is defining a boundary for the couple—e.g., we are dating exclusively, we are committed, who is invited to the wedding.

Couples with boundary problems include refusing to give up old romances, unwilling to commit or inviting your family on your honeymoon. The process of becoming "we" or "us" is often a long one but the key is for the couple to take priority and continue those relationships with family and friends that are positive and rewarding.

The birth of the first child is an event that can produce closeness or distance for each couple. Couples lose privacy, sleep, leisure time, sexuality and resources at this special time. Often the infant becomes such a focus or even preoccupation that one or both spouses feel ignored. Research shows infancy is the time of lowest marital satisfaction for normal couples so, it is very important for the couple to take time for their own needs during this period. This is also a good time for self-disclosure of beliefs and ideas about parenting and an opportunity to learn together.

8. SELF-DISCLOSE YOUR PERSONAL CONSTRUCTS.
a) Verbally
b) Revealing
c) How you construe
d) Your parents' relationships
e) Your past relationships
f) Your current relationships
g) Honesty
h) To your partner

EXPRESSIVENESS

Self-disclosure is the process of verbally revealing your thoughts, feelings, needs and experience to another person. Self-disclosure is just ONE aspect of a couple's communication skills. BUT, self-disclosure is the single aspect of communication that determines closeness in a relationship.

PREVIOUSLY, we discussed how important the process of self-disclosure is during courtship. Self-disclosure allows us the opportunity to get to know whether someone we are attracted to has similar values and attitudes that will contribute to compatibility.

In CLOSE relationships self-disclosure is reciprocal with both spouses revealing thoughts and feelings equally. This process contributes to a greater understanding. As the process continues these self-disclosures will increase in depth and privacy regarding experiences seldom shared in social relationships. Self-disclosure contributes to the development of trust and acceptance.

Of course, other communication skills are also important. Close relationships are characterized by good listening skills. The ability to listen attentively and empathetically encourages increased self-disclosure. The expression of thoughts and feelings which are CONGRUENT with nonverbal communication is also characteristic of good marriages. Once again couples must make time for meaningful communication. Couples with close relationships make sure to turn off the TV, radio, cell-phone in order to have "up close and personal" conversations. We used that phrase because sadly today some couples know more about the likes and habits of celebrities than they do about their own spouse.

So one of the KEYS to developing a closer relationship is to gradually reveal your private self to your spouse at the same time as you make time to develop your listening skills to try to get to know and understand your spouse.

SOME CLOSING REMARKS

Hopefully, if this little book has been successful, you have a better understanding of intimacy, where you stand as close or distant in your marriage (or relationship), and what you might choose to do next.

I thought I would share with you some characteristics of couples I have had the pleasure of observing move from distant to close relationships with the help of some counseling. These couples are honest with themselves and their spouses. In spite of their discord they genuinely care about one another. They have a psychological flexibility and interpersonal curiosity. They are accountable for their own contribution to the distance in their marriage. They don't just read this book—they study and reflect. They respond to opportunity and challenge and they are WILLING TO CHANGE.

We hope you will choose

A CLOSE, CONFIDING RELATIONSHIP.

Abstract

Enhancing Marital Intimacy Therapy (EMIT) is a cognitive marital therapy designed to enhance marital intimacy through a structured process of self-disclosure of personal constructs. The maintenance of inaccurate personal constructs is identified as a major obstacle to the development of intimacy between individuals and is presented as the rationale behind couple pathology. The role of therapy is then to encourage the disclosure of these faulty schema in order to foster mutual understanding between spouses and thus facilitate the enhancement of marital intimacy. A summary of how EMIT is implemented and practiced in the clinical setting is presented. Outcome and process based research aimed at determining the effectiveness of the EMIT approach is described. Enhancing Marital Intimacy Therapy is offered as a humane, efficient, and effective technique of marital therapy.

Introduction

E nhancing Marital Intimacy Therapy (EMIT) is a cognitive marital therapy designed to enhance marital intimacy through a structured process of self-disclosure of personal constructs (1). This approach is grounded on the assertion that the bond between husband and wife is the single thread that explains successful marriages and strong families (2). The maintenance of inaccurate personal constructs is identified as a major obstacle to the development of intimacy between individuals and is presented as the rationale behind couple pathology. The role of therapy is then to encourage the disclosure of these faulty schema in order to foster mutual understanding between spouses and thus facilitate the enhancement of marital intimacy.

What is intimacy? Intimate relationships are considered to be the most important kind of interpersonal relationships. They are felt most deeply. They provide a unique sense of attachment and belonging. Marital intimacy is not just the sum of two independently acting individuals but is a mix of two personalities which as a *dyad* has qualities not present in the actions of the isolated spouses. Erikson (3) suggests that the development of intimacy is the major psychosocial task of young adulthood. The behavioral aspect of intimacy is predictability; the emotional aspect is a feeling of closeness; the cognitive aspect is understanding through self-disclosure; and the attitudinal aspect is commitment.

Intimacy is one of three psychological dimensions which can describe the quality of interpersonal relationships (6). "Boundary" and "power" are the other two psychological dimensions. *Boundary* refers to the couple's relationships in time and space to other individuals and social units. *Power* refers to the couple's capacity to resolve their conflicting needs and the style they use to resolve such differences.

Intimacy has been found to be the interpersonal dimension in marriage which contributes most to marital adjustment (4, 5). The study of intimacy has been facilitated by the development of an operational definition of marital intimacy (7, 8) and a self-report questionnaire that is designed to provide valid and reliable assessment of the following eight facets of marital quality: conflict resolution, affection, cohesion, sexuality, identity, compatibility, autonomy, and expressiveness (9). Research results have demonstrated that a lack of marital intimacy is associated with both marital maladjustment as well as families which are enmeshed and chaotic (10). Thus a therapeutic approach which could enhance marital intimacy should, in theory, improve marital adjustment and family functioning.

A Cognitive View of Marital Intimacy

If mutual understanding is considered one of the defining aspects of marital intimacy, it can be reasoned that problems within the marriage related to a lack of intimacy may at least in part be cognitive in nature. The cognitive aspects of relationship distress have received increased recognition by a variety of professionals with an interest in understanding and treating marital discord (17). This can be largely credited to a revival of George Kelly's cognitive view of personality by academic psychologists with an interest in a cognitive view of psychotherapy (18, 19).

Kelly believed that the essence of human life is the anticipation of experience. He proposed a theory of personality based on the concept of personal constructs (20) and defined it as the characteristic conceptual model employed by an individual to interpret events and make predictions about the future. These personal constructs are the cherished belief systems that each of us use to make sense of the world around us. Indeed, Kelly viewed every man, woman and child as an amateur scientist, one who develops a personal theory about one's experience and then sets out to establish a rigorous proof. Through our interactions with others, each person is constantly testing these personal constructs which are then either modified, abandoned or maintained, depending on the outcome they elicit. When considering a partner in marriage Kelly observed that, "a man will choose to marry if that appears to provide him with the opportunity to enlarge or secure his anticipatory system" (p. 5). With regard to marital relationships, our personal constructs serve us by enabling us to elaborate upon and confirm our experiences with our partners. According to Segraves (21), intimacy occurs when partners have many complex, flexible personal constructs on which to draw, while marital discord is the consequence of a few simple, rigid personal constructs.

Consistent with this assertion, Neimeyer (24) suggests that marital dissatisfaction can be viewed as a breakdown in an ongoing cooperation between spouses to understand the relationship due to a contradiction between one's personal construct system and the evidence at hand. This idea suggests that couples can only enjoy their role as husband or wife in the light of how they construe the behavior of their spouse. In the absence of sufficient understanding, marital discord is likely. Narrow and rigid personal constructs not only distort interactions between spouses but also limit the elaboration of their experience as a couple. If spouses refuse to acknowledge or accept one another's different views of their experience, the constant revision of each spouse's personal construct system, thought to be vital to successful marriages, will become static. Hostility in marriage, therefore, may be the result of both spouses insisting on maintaining narrow and rigid personal constructs. As Kelly observed, certain personal constructs are likely to persist in the face of considerable counterevidence (p. 95).

Self-Disclosure as the Key to Understanding

Self-disclosure refers to the process of making the private self known to others. Cognitive self-disclosure refers to revealing one's ideas, attitudes, beliefs and theories regarding one's relationships and behavior. Cognitive self-disclosure is thus differentiated from emotional self-disclosure which is revealing one's feelings, an approach that often produces distance rather than closeness. An early study by Waring reported that couples believe self-disclosure to be an important component of marital intimacy (9). Indeed, the exchange of such information about one's inner self is considered to be the major process through which closeness between people develops (11).

Sidney Jourard (9), in his book *The Transparent Self*, stated that a choice that confronts us at every moment is this: "Shall we permit our fellow persons to know us as we are, or shall we seek instead to remain an enigma, an uncertain quality, wishing to be seen as something we are not?" (p.3) Jourard wondered whether there was some connection between his clients' needs to consult with a professional psychotherapist and their reluctance to be known by their spouses and families.

Jourard commented that, "Husbands and wives are strangers one to the other to an incredible degree" (p. 4). He described a happily married—something he thought was altogether rare: "They know each other, care for and about one another, respond to the needs, actions and emotions of the other, and respect each other's idiosyncrasies and uniqueness" (p. 31). He suggested that, in our society, people many in a romantic haze, usually ignorant of the thoughts, feelings and aims of their future spouse, partly as a result of deliberate ambiguity or contrivance on the part of the other.

According to Jourard, the consequence of disclosing one's inner thoughts, feelings, and wants is that one learns: 1) the extent to which one is similar to another; 2) to understand the other person's needs; and 3) the extent to which the other person accords with or deviates from one's own value system and from moral and ethical standards. He hinted that an individual's self-disclosing behavior might be a product of how one's childhood disclosures were met in the family of origin—some ignored, some rewarded, some punished. Jourard suggested that in marriage one withdraws self-disclosure from the family of origin for increased self-disclosure with the spouse. He proposed that "healthy personalities" are people who not only play their roles satisfactorily, but also derive personal satisfaction from role enactment and are able to disclose themselves in some optimum degree to at least one significant other.

Jourard's insight that the process of self-disclosure was critical to the development of marital intimacy has led to considerable research on self-disclosure and marriage (12, 13, 14, 15, 16, 17, 18). Surprisingly, only a handful of marital therapists have specifically focused on spouses' self-disclosing behavior as a possibly effective counselling technique (22, 23).

The Therapist's Role

Neimeyer (22) has summarized the therapist's role as one of facilitating the self-disclosure of personal constructs. When the therapist encourages a distressed couple to articulate beliefs, attitudes and ideas about the relationship and the implications thereof, it frequently becomes apparent that spouses share dissimilar understandings of presenting issues. Segraves (21) explains that each spouse enters the marriage with certain beliefs about the form marriage should take and about the role of husband or wife. He suggests that these personal constructs are learned through the precedent set by the family of origin, from previous close relationships and the cultural norm. Discrepancy in these beliefs between spouses is a source of conflict while similarity in beliefs facilitates marital adjustment.

Segraves argues that chronic marital discord is a consequence of both spouses' fixated way of misconstruing their partner's character and motivation.

He believes that this is a direct consequence of either spouse having only a few narrow and rigid personal constructs upon which to draw, as well as a habitual cognitive structure that is low in cognitive complexity—often pinpointed as traits such as being rigid, insensitive, opinionated, or stubborn. Segraves sees the therapist's task as one of facilitating greater cognitive complexity in each individual by helping couples to increase self-disclosure, considering alternative explanations or constructs, and accepting the spouse's behavior as discrepant from their expectations—a cognitive decision Kelly described as "constructive alternativism."

In summary, it is proposed that therapy aimed at facilitating successful marriages and strong families should focus on increasing self-disclosure of personal constructs and fostering greater cognitive complexity through the consideration of construct alternatives as a means to enhance marital intimacy. It is the assertion of this author that EMIT is ideally designed for just such a challenge.

PRACTICE

Assessment (The Marital Intimacy Assessment Interview)

The assessment interview begins with introductions and attempts on the part of the interviewer to develop rapport with the couple by asking such questions as how they feel about disclosing information about their relationship. The interviewer inquires as to how the decision to seek help was made. Finally, the interviewer may ask neutral questions about years of marriage, number of children, living arrangements, and source of referral.

Step 1: The Presenting Problem

A brief exploration of each spouse's perceptions of the presenting problem is a neutral method of starting the session and gives the therapist an opportunity to evaluate whether there is agreement. The most commonly cited interpersonal problems are persistent arguments, drifting apart, poor communication, and a recent affair or separation. Occasionally, the presenting problem is a specific trait or behavior which one spouse finds distressing.

This is the point at which the marital intimacy assessment interview departs from other evaluation models. As little as five minutes is spent on the presenting problem mainly because the presenting issue is usually poorly understood as well as being the focus for negative feelings, self-justification, and projection. Evidence suggests strongly that the expression of negative feelings at such an early point in the assessment leads to distance between spouses (7).

Each spouse's theory on why the presenting problem exists is elicited next. They are asked, for example, why arguments occur in their relationship. If they have no specific ideas that relate to themselves, they may be asked how arguments occur in other relationships that they are familiar with or in couples in general. The questions or use of standard probes such as, "What is your theory on why you argue about money?" initiates the process of self-disclosure of personal constructs. The spouses' theories are often quite discrepant. This segment will usually require five to ten minutes.

Step 2: Attraction, Dating, Courtship

The couple is asked about how they met and why they were attracted to each other. As well as giving information about conscious factors in partner choice, this allows an assessment of the degree of psychological-mindedness of the couple while recalling the most positively remembered aspect of their relationship. These questions also take the couple away, from the anger and the frustration of the presenting problem. The information is always interesting ranging from blind dates, chance meetings, high school romances to arranged marriages. Distressed couples are often unable to verbalize the attributes which attracted them to their future spouse. The couples are asked about their families' reactions to their spouses. Questions about courtship, engagement, and the wedding follow. This segment requires ten to fifteen minutes and continues the process of self-disclosure.

Step 3: Parents' Level of Intimacy

During the next ten minutes, the couple is asked to describe their observations and experiences with their parents' marriage. This is often the first time they have been asked to articulate their perceptions of the quality of their parents' relationship. Spouses often describe persistent arguments, lack of affection, sleeping in separate bedrooms, divorce or separation, alcoholism, and a variety of other specific problems. One consistent observation is that one parent's behavior is often blamed for the parents' marital problems, and the client is unable to present an explanation as to the other parent's contribution to the problem. Often the other spouse is able to describe facets of their in-laws' marriage which the client is unable to describe.

Both spouses are asked their thoughts on how these examples of marital discord affected them personally. The common response is that they made a promise to themselves not to repeat the problems or that they wished to avoid marrying a person like the parent they perceived as contributing most to the discord. Most couples report that this is the first time they have disclosed some of this information to their spouse. This process allows the interviewer to make an assessment of the couple's interpersonal curiosity.

Step 4: Marital Lifecycle

A chronological history of the marriage is now taken starting from the honeymoon. This will often allow a neutral introduction to any specific sexual problems. The birth of children and the couple's ideas of how this influenced their relationship is explored. During this phase, the couple will often identify the point at which they first perceived dissatisfaction with the marriage and why they believed discord was developing. Couples may identify problems with establishing boundaries for the relationship in the early years relating to premarital pregnancies, over-involvement with family of origin or an unwillingness to give up a previous lifestyle. Problems encountered from three to five years of marriage usually revolve around issues of power such as career decisions, living arrangements, or child care. Issues of intimacy often surface from five to seven years and are commonly referred to as the "seven-year itch." Parenting problems are often encountered during the next ten to twenty years, followed by issues of boredom or the empty nest. Specific issues of illness, unemployment, remarriage, and emotional illness may be revealed. This segment lasts about ten minutes.

Step 5: Current Relationship

In this ten-minute segment, we bring the couple back to the present by evaluating their current relationship in terms of the eight aspects of intimacy described by Waring, et al. (7, 8). How do you as a couple express affection? How committed are you to this relationship? How do you attempt to resolve differences of opinion? How do you get along sexually together? What is the communication like between you? How do you get along with family, children, and friends? How compatible are you as a couple? How do you feel you compare to other couples? Both spouses are given an opportunity to respond to each question and their style of responding is observed allowing comparison to other couples who respond to this rather structured section.

Step 6: Feedback, Evaluation, Therapy Contract

The interviewer will now spend about ten minutes providing feedback about the presenting problem, the relationship of the presenting problem to issues of spouse selection, the influence of the parents' marriage, and issues raised from the history and current status of the relationship. The feedback is usually positive and negative. For example, "The problem of persistent unresolved arguments was present during courtship, but you believed it would stop after your wedding in spite of growing up with arguments on both sides of the family. Currently arguments over your marriage roles persist in spite of a lot of affection, compatibility, and commitment." The couple is asked whether they agree or disagree with these observations.

The therapist proceeds by explaining the notion that closeness between spouses is the single thread which explains successful marriages and strong families. They are introduced to the concept that experience and research suggest that couples often experience a lack of closeness. While this does not necessarily cause marital discord, sessions designed to help couples disclose more of their beliefs about their relationship may enhance marital intimacy. It is explained that the therapist will try to help them understand the reasons behind the presenting conflict by exploring their own theories on the influence of their parents' marriage, their motivation for choosing their spouse and their ideas about the relationship.

Nine out of ten couples at least tentatively accept this model and agree to participate in ten one-hour sessions of self-disclosure of personal constructs. The format of the sessions is described to the couple and they are asked to complete three self-report questionnaires for evaluation purposes before the second session. These include the General Health Questionnaire (a measure of symptoms of non-psychotic emotional illness), the Locke-Wallace Marital Adjustment Scale, and the Waring Intimacy Questionnaire (25, 26, 9).

Certainly there are couples who do not accept the applicability of the theory of disclosure of personal constructs to their own marriage and thus do not agree to a treatment contract. Some couples do not wish to participate in self-disclosure but rather would prefer specific advice on how to approach impasses, opinions about whether the marriage is viable, specific prescriptions of recommended behavioral changes, or a focus on the here and now.

Finally, the therapist seeks the couples' opinions about the initial assessment. The majority disclose that it was not what they had expected, that the disclosures were interesting and novel, and that they were hopeful about the therapy. Often couples express amazement about how similar their problems are to their parents' problems. It is at this point in the assessment interview that the couple is encouraged to participate in setting up a treatment contract. The purpose of the contract is to clearly define the goals of therapy with a particular couple, to specify the method that will be employed to attempt to achieve those goals, and to lay down the ground rules for how each party will conduct themselves during therapy. Usually the rules for conduct include an agreement by both parties to: restrict disclosures to ideas, beliefs and attitudes rather than feelings; that emotional outbursts such as weeping, manipulative tactics, and hostile overtures are to be suppressed as they may inhibit disclosure or impair listening; interruptions of self-disclosures are not permitted; and that the couple direct their disclosures to the therapist and not to each other.

Indications and Contraindications
The success of Enhancing Marital Intimacy Therapy is closely tied to proper patient selection. Those who will benefit from EMIT are couples who lack

intimacy in their relationship, are inhibited in self-disclosure and employ few inflexible and erroneous personal constructs to interpret their spouse's behavior. Indeed, these three key concepts provide the very theoretical underpinnings of EMIT. This technique is not designed for couples where one or both suffer from substance abuse, a severe affective disorder, or a psychotic emotional illness (24, 27). The couple's interest and active participation during the assessment interview is predictive of good compliance with the EMIT protocol and an involved approach in therapy sessions. The use of the Waring Intimacy Questionnaire, the Locke-Wallace Marital Adjustment Scale, and the General Health Questionnaire will enhance appropriate patient selection and provide a baseline for more formal evaluation of outcomes at the conclusion of therapy.

Treatment (Enhancing Marital Intimacy Therapy)
Enhancing Marital Intimacy Therapy is a structured, time-limited intervention designed to facilitate the self-disclosure of personal constructs (2). This technique reduces symptoms of non-psychotic emotional illness, improves some aspects of marital adjustment, and enhances marital intimacy. It can be summarized by instructing therapists to comply in a standardized fashion with the following nine guidelines:

EMIT PROTOCOL

Therapist Actions

1) Explanations of Sessions and Treatment Contract Therapy begins with an explanation of the treatment contract. This will include a statement of the aim of therapy, the method to be employed, and an emphasis on the importance of prohibiting interruptions during self-disclosure. The session starts with the therapist stating, "We will be meeting for ten sessions over a ten-week period. During the sessions I will ask you a series of questions designed to help you understand why your relationship is not as close as you both wish. During the sessions you agree not to interrupt your spouse while he (or she) attempts to answer the questions. I will turn to each spouse in an alternating pattern and ask, 'What were you thinking?' The questions will be about your marriage and your parents' and grandparents' relationships. If there are interruptions, I will terminate the session. If you both agree, we can commence the session or I will answer any questions you may wish to ask."

2) Initiation of First and Subsequent Sessions
The presenting problem revealed in the assessment interview provides the impetus for the initial question of the first session. For example, if a self-disclosure in the interview produced the theme of persistent arguments as the presenting problem, the therapist would lead off the first session with the question, "What is your theory of why you and your spouse argue so frequently?"
Each spouse's disclosure of personal constructs is stimulated by the standard probe, "What were you thinking while your spouse was talking?" Self-disclosure can be facilitated by nondirective questions such as "Go on" and "Tell me more" until the patient says, "I don't know," or three to five minutes go by. The first question of each subsequent session should be the last unanswered question of the previous session.

3) Facilitating Cognitive Self-Disclosure
The therapist should assist the couple in clarifying their thoughts, beliefs, attitudes, and opinions. The standard probe, "What were you thinking while your spouse was talking?" is the cornerstone of facilitating cognitive self-disclosure and is instrumental to avoiding the discussion of feelings which often produce distance between spouses. In addition, many people use the word "feel" when they are revealing a

thought, "I feel my wife is exaggerating." It is the therapist's role to assist them in recognizing this is not a "feeling" but rather an opinion. The therapist should find as many ways to encourage self-disclosure as possible. Each spouse should speak in turn through the therapist, commenting upon each other's disclosures and giving additional information when necessary.

4) Clarification
Following a spouse's disclosure, the therapist may assist in the clarification of ambiguous theories, beliefs, and values through nondirective questioning, relabeling, or rephrasing thoughts. Nondirective questions may include "Tell me more about your thoughts" and "Could you explain more about your beliefs?" Rephrasing involves putting the patient's thoughts into briefer and clearer words such as "You think women are inconsistent."

5) Redirection
The therapist should redirect the attention of spouses to the discussion at hand, when warranted, or to personal constructs which they have previously disclosed and that are relevant to the present focus. For example, the therapist may ask the husband, "What were you thinking while your wife was talking?" to which he responds, "I was thinking about the parking meter." The therapist should redirect the husband back to the core question for the couple, "What did you think about your wife's thought about loneliness as a motive for marriage?"

6) Nondirective Questions
Therapists should use nondirective questions to encourage disclosure of personal constructs as much as possible because the core of the therapy is the couple's self-disclosure as a "process" rather than the therapist's ideas of which issues are significant.

7) Parents' Marriages
The therapist should encourage the couple to think about their parents' marriages and the constructs that developed as a result of those observations and experience with their family of origin. This is especially warranted when there are questions they are unable to answer such as with, "I don't know why we argue so frequently."

8) Grandparents, Friends, and Other Couples
This exploration should be extended to the marriages of grandparents, friends, and their previous relationships when appropriate. The therapist any ask, "Do you have any theories on why your grandmother married an alcoholic?"

9) Therapist Theories

After listening to the couple for several weeks, the therapist may develop some theories about the relationship distress which may be presented as material for discussion. For example, the therapist may say, "I have a theory that the good opinion of your children is more important than your own closeness. What do you think about my theory?"

Therapist Non-actions
The EMIT protocol includes the following five things not to do:

1) Feelings

The therapist should not allow outbursts of emotion to interfere with the self-disclosure process. The therapist should suppress the tendency of some spouses to react emotionally through tears, arguments and ultimatums. Feelings of sadness or anger and related behaviors should not be allowed to become the focus of therapy or to be utilized as resistances to inhibit a spouse from honestly disclosing. Instead, the therapist should focus on patients' cognitive theories of why they reacted in a specific way or why they feel sad or angry.

2) Mind Reading

The therapist should always remember that the major task is cognitive and self-disclosure. The therapist should identify and suppress the common tendency of couples to use projection and self-justification such as "My husband thinks I'm useless" or "Of course, I keep things from my wife since the affair." "Why do you think you married someone whom you perceive belittles you?" is one example or redirecting such material to its conscious, cognitive components.

3) Behavior

The therapist should not identify, confront, or comment on the couple's nonverbal behaviors with comments such as, "I notice that you appear bored with this process." These behaviors, if they are thought to be interfering with the process of cognitive self-disclosure, should be identified only as a violation of the treatment contract.

4) Interaction

All interruptions should be noted for the content of the self-disclosure is usually quite revealing and even crucial for understanding the couple's conflict. However, the therapist should take control and stop arguments, interruptions, and talkativeness. If interruptions continue following a warning, the session should be discontinued.

5) Resistances

Do not attempt to interpret resistances. If both members of the couple no longer wish to mutually disclose, their wishes should be respected and the sessions terminated. If only one spouse does not wish to continue, the reasons should be explored but only if material disclosed can be revealed to the spouse in the next session.

EFFICACY

Research aimed at determining the usefulness of any particular therapy will usually attempt first to demonstrate the intervention's effectiveness at bringing about the desired outcome and secondly to determine the processes through which a particular outcome is achieved.

Outcome-Based Research Effectiveness refers to whether the therapy is better than no therapy. Comparison to waiting-list controls or to a gold standard of marital therapy outcome is the ideal measure of efficacy. Many studies make use of both subjective and objective measures of change. The difficulties with subjective ratings have been discussed frequently in the literature but do provide the clinical reality of evaluation for therapist and patient (28).

Enhancing Marital Intimacy Therapy (EMIT) is based on the notion that closeness between husband and wife is the single thread that explains successful marriages and strong families. The self-disclosure of personal constructs between spouses is a unique approach designed to enhance marital intimacy and improve marital functioning. The ideal study of EMIT's effectiveness would demonstrate statistically significant increases in subjective and/or objective measures of marital functioning and satisfaction as a result of therapy when compared to a control. It would achieve this end through the mechanism that its name purports; that is to say, the ideal study would clearly establish that self-disclosure of personal constructs increases, that this causes intimacy in marriages to increase, and that this is the reason behind improved marital functioning.

The intrinsic difficulties associated with designing and implementing an intervention in a clinical population makes even the approximation of the ideal extremely challenging. The reality is that withholding active treatment as a control measure is viewed as unethical and attrition with waiting list controls is common. With this in mind, a series of outcome studies is presented demonstrating the effectiveness of cognitive self-disclosure as an approach to marital therapy for some but not all couples.

An uncontrolled outcome study by Waring and Russel (29) examined the role that self-disclosure of personal constructs might play in the treatment of distressed families. Cognitive Family Therapy (CFT), as it is termed in this context, attempted to treat family pathology through focusing on increasing intimacy between the spouses. The sample was a difficult heterogeneous treatment group consisting of eleven families of whom: 1) some individuals had moderate to severe psychiatric illness; 2) none had been referred for family therapy; and 3) the majority had previous psychiatric treatment and were referred as treatment failures. This heterogeneous group is presented because of the importance of evaluating therapies in real clinical settings, and the results have implications for this approach in difficult patient populations. Results from objective self-report tests given pre and post-treatment found that neurotic symptomatology was improved by 80 percent which is above usually reported spontaneous improvement rates during the ten weeks of therapy. In 45 percent of these cases participation in CFT was associated with improvement in marital adjustment and 88 percent improvement in family functioning. Despite the fact that objective tests demonstrated increased cohesion, improved compatibility for affection, increased expressiveness, decreased conflict and improved marital adjustment, no conclusions could be drawn regarding the role of intimacy and self-disclosure in CFT as the results were not statistically significant, and the hypothesis not directly tested. The results did however suggest that further evaluation was warranted.

In a randomized clinical trial of Cognitive Marital Therapy (CMT) by Waring, Carver, et al. (30), thirty-three couples with severe marital discord referred to a psychiatric outpatient department were assigned to either CMT or a control therapy that involved sessions of self-disclosure from a programmed marital enhancement text with inexperienced therapists. Personal distress, marital adjustment, marital intimacy, and aspects of self-disclosure were measured before and after treatment. Symptoms of depression as well as somatic and compulsive complaints showed significant improvement for both groups. The wives exhibited a trend that suggested they were making more self-disclosures to their spouses after counseling. However, no significant differences were found between the marital therapy group and the control group. Marital intimacy and marital satisfaction did not improve significantly over the course of ten therapy sessions. This may have reflected unique features of the sample whose mean pre-therapy scores on the Waring Intimacy Questionnaire were surprisingly similar to population mean scores, suggesting a possible restricted range of variance from pre to post-therapy outcome scores. The study did suggest a trend toward increased self-disclosure by wives as being associated with symptom relief. Further evaluation of the role of self-disclosure in marital therapy was indicated.

A waiting list controlled trial of CMT in the treatment of severe marital discord was

embarked upon by Waring, Stalker, et al. (31). The study found that there was no spontaneous remission in marital discord in couples on the ten-week waiting list control group and almost half of these couples dropped out of the study altogether suggesting that waiting lists are not

appropriate as controls for marital therapy research. Subjective and objective evaluations

revealed interesting outcomes. For the twenty-nine couples for whom data was available, 83 percent reported feeling "better of" for having had the therapy experience. Therapists rated 56 percent of couples as improved as a result of the therapy. Couples in therapy and on the waiting list showed a significant reduction in symptoms of nonpsychotic emotional illness. However, no significant reduction in measures of marital discord were found in comparison to the control group despite improvement in conflict resolution scores and problem-solving communication found for the CMT group. The fact that there was a significant pattern of improvement on nine relevant outcome measures for females in the therapy group in comparison to females in the waiting list condition was encouraging. The authors concluded that therapeutic self-disclosure of personal constructs may provide some subjective and objective relief in some women with severe marital discord.

Finally, in a review of three controlled outcome studies Waring (32) examines the effectiveness of EMIT, alone or in combination with antidepressant medication, for treatment of women with moderate to severe depression. The studies suggest that EMIT in combination with antidepressant medication is not indicated for hospitalized women with major affective disorder but either alone or in combination with antidepressants, EMIT is a viable treatment for outpatient women who are suffering from dysthymic disorder. Dandenau et al compared EMIT to "Emotionally Focused Therapy" which is based on attachment theory and involves self-disclosure of feelings. Both were found to be effective in the short term with EFT having better long term results. (33).

Process-Based Research Process research in marital therapy can be viewed as the study of interactions between the couple and the therapist while treatment is still in progress (33). Process research is concerned with "how" couples change. Process research seeks answers to questions about the inner workings of marital therapy (34, 35). This section will focus on research aimed at elucidating those aspects of self-disclosure of personal constructs that are associated with therapeutic change and discuss implications for the practice of marital and family therapy in general.

Amount of Self-Disclosure

A positive relationship between the amount of self-disclosure and marital satisfaction has consistently been demonstrated. For example, Davidson, Blaswick, and Halverson (13) found that spouses who report more self-disclosure in their marriage tend to report greater marital adjustment. Waring and Chelune (14) found that self-disclosing behavior, as measured by the Self-Disclosing Coding System (SDCS), is a major determinant of various aspects of marital intimacy. To state that good marriages are characterized by greater amounts of self-disclosure than are poor marriages is obviously only a description and not necessarily an explanation of how healthy marriages develop. However, the EMIT approach is based on the assumption that increasing the amount of self-disclosure between spouses of their thoughts, memories, and concepts about relationships will improve the quality of their marriage.

Some cautionary comments and explanation about precisely what is meant by "increasing the amount" of self-disclosure seem indicated. In the ideal courtship, self-disclosure of memories about relationships, expectations about marriage, and attitudes toward the opposite sex occurs spontaneously as the couple gets to know each other. Marital discord may be a consequence of neurotic withholding or deliberate contrivance on the part of spouses who fail to disclose about their genuine self. When these couples are asked in therapy to discuss motives that may have been withheld for five, ten, or twenty years, these revelations may cause suffering and stimulate re-evaluation of their commitment to marriage. Thus, self-disclosure of personal constructs has the potential to produce painful insights. Nevertheless, this understanding does allow spouses the choice of accepting the relationship as flawed, redefining the relationship on a more authentic basis, or terminating the relationship.

Reciprocity of Self-Disclosure

Research has consistently demonstrated that marital adjustment is related to a factor described by various authors as "reciprocity," "equity," "compatibility," and "homogamy." This factor of "reciprocity" is descriptive of good relationships. Perhaps not surprisingly then, reciprocity of self-disclosure between spouses has also been found to be positively associated with marital adjustment. Hansen and Schuldt (15) found that couples with discrepancies in the amount of self-disclosure output reported less marital satisfaction. Davidson et al. (13) found that the greater the discrepancy in a partner's self-disclosure of feelings, the less was the spouse's perception of marital adjustment. The factor of reciprocity may also be descriptive of good marital therapy. Thus, the self-disclosure of personal constructs has been designed to provide reciprocity of the amount, kind, and depth of self-disclosure.

Social exchange theory supports the idea that a balance between partners in therapy may be necessary. According to the principle of social exchange, we consciously review the costs and rewards of our relationships, and if the rewards outweigh the costs, the relationship will continue. Thus, reciprocity of self-disclosure can be conceived as rewarding if both spouses provide explanations that help explain their discord and offer opportunity for change; revealing weaknesses and insecurities are perceived as equal costs by the couple.

Depth of Self-Disclosure

During the natural course of a relationship, breadth of self-disclosure is typically greater in the initial stage while depth of self-disclosure increases as the relationship continues to develop over a period of time. Waterman (16) has reviewed studies suggesting that marital satisfaction is related to the depth of self-disclosures and the relevance of the material.

Several consequences of increasing the amount of self-disclosure in marital therapy can also be clarified. Usually, as the amount of self-disclosure increases, the disclosures themselves will be of a more personal and private nature. The expectations, memories, and attitudes revealed become more psychologically sophisticated. A recent study by Waring, Schaeffer, and Fry (37) demonstrated a positive association between changes in the depth of disclosures and increases in perceived marital intimacy as a result of couples' participation in EMIT.

Ego Relevance of Disclosures

As remarked upon earlier, Waterman (16) has reviewed research that supports the idea that the perceived relevance of material being disclosed in a relationship is an important determinant of a couple's marital satisfaction.

Some therapeutic approaches allow couples to disclose their attitudes about politics, religion, or nuclear war, hardly relevant to their current concerns. Yet what appears to be most relevant to the development of a close, confiding relationship in marriage is the personal constructs children develop, between the ages of four and fifteen, to explain their experience and observation of their parents' marriage (5). These thoughts are conscious and available for self-disclosure. Couples can report memories of how their parents expressed affection; how their parents attempted to resolve differences of opinion; and how they communicated with each other. The problems they describe in their parents' marriages are frequently mirrored in their own relationship. Thus they find self-disclosure of personal constructs about their parents' marriages to be innovative, interesting, and relevant to understanding their own marital discord.

Disclosure Patterns

Future Lines of Research Questions related to whether therapeutic change is a direct consequence of disclosure of personal constructs or is simply a result of improved communication skills have yet to be answered. Do alterations in personal constructs have to occur in order for there to be a therapeutic benefit or is simply understanding "why" sufficient to enhance marital functioning? What personal constructs, if any, are most relevant to marital discord? Does "constructive alternativism" take more than ten sessions?

Clinical experience with couples who have participated in Enhancing Marital Intimacy Therapy suggests some possibilities yet clearly the role of personal constructs in marital therapy needs to be studied more directly. One potential direction would be the measurement of personal constructs directly before and after therapy in order to evaluate whether alterations have occurred. Technically this is feasible using techniques such as the reparatory grid (20).

A second direction is the more direct measurement of the constructs that children develop in response to the marital discord of their parents should be studied and prospectively evaluated to identify the influence on personality and relationship development. While most couples accept the relevance of these observations for therapy, it is not yet clear whether they are really meaningful. The kind, number, and flexibility of personal constructs in marital maladjustment deserve further study.

Summary

E nhancing Marital Intimacy Therapy (EMIT) is a brief structured marital therapy based on self-disclosure of personal constructs. The approach is grounded on the notion that the closeness between husband and wife is the single thread that explains successful marriages and strong families. The role of therapy is to enhance intimacy by facilitating the self-disclosure of how each spouse construes the current discord based on their own cherished theories of how relationships operate. Outcome studies have demonstrated the effectiveness of this approach for some but not all couples. Process based studies support the idea that increasing the amount and depth of positive disclosures of personally relevant material in a reciprocal fashion between spouses in a disturbed marriage is a technique that will enhance intimacy and thus increase marital satisfaction. Whether personal constructs must change in order for therapy to be effective remains to be determined. EMIT appears to be a humane, efficient, and effective technique for the treatment of marital discord.

References

1. Waring,E.M.,Enhancing Marital Intimacy Through Facilitating Cognitive Self-Disclosure,New York,Brunner/Mazel,1988.
2. Berman,E.M.,Lief, H.I., Marital Therapy from a Psychiatric Perspective:An Overview,American Journal of Psychiatry,132:583-592.
3. Erikson,E.H. (1950) Childhood and Society (2nd edition). W.W.Norton Co.,New York.
4. Beavers,W.R. (1985) Sucessful Marriage: A Family Systems Approach to Couples Therapy.New York,W.W.Norton.
5. Stinnett, N. (1985) Strong Families (p304-314) in Marriage and Family In A Changing Society. (Second Edition). Edited by Henslin, J.M., New York, The Free Press.
6. Brehm, S.S. (1985). Intimate Relationships. New York, Random House.
7. Hinde, R.A. (1978), Interpersonal Relationships- In Quest of a Science, Psychological Medicine, Vol 3, p 378-386.
8. Waring, E. M., Tillmann, M. P., Frelick, L., Russell, L., Weisz, G. (1980). Concepts of Intimacy in the General Population, JNMD 168(8):471-474. Ile reces 32
9. Waring, E. M., McElrath, D., Lefcoe, D., Weisz, G. (1981). Dimensions of Intimacy in Marriage. Psychiatry, 44(2):169-175.
10. Waring, E. M., McElrath, D., Mitchell, P., Derry, M.E. (1981). Intimacy and Emotional Illness in the General Population. Canadian Psychiatric Journal, 26:167-17.
11. Waring, E. M. (1984). The Measurement of Marital Intimacy. Journal of Marital and Family Therapy, 10(2):185-192.
12. Brown, G. W., Harris, T. (1978). Social Origins of Depression: A Study of Psychiatric Disorder in Women. London, Free Press.
13. Henderson, S. (1980). A Development in Social Psychiatry — The Systematic Study of Social Bonds. JNMD. 168(2):63-69.

14. Patton, D., Waring, E. M. (1984). The Quality and Quantity of Marital Intimacy in the Marriages of Psychiatric Patients. Journal Sexual Marital Therapy._ 10(3):201-206.
15. Waring, E. M., Chamberlaine, C. H., McCrank, E. W., Carver, C., Stalker, C., Fry, R. (1989). Intimacy and Help-Seeking. Canadian Journal of Psychiatry.
16. Waring, E. M., Patton, D. (1984). Marital Intimacy and Family Functioning. The Psychiatric Journal of the University of Ottawa, 9(1):24-29.
17. Henderson. S., Byrne D. G., Duncan-Jones , P. (1981). Neurosis and the Social Environment., New York, Academic Press.
18. Waring, E. M., Patton, D., Wister, A.V. (1990). The Etiology of Nonpsychotic Emotional Illness. Canadian Psychiatric Journal, 35(1):50-57.
19. Jourard, S.M. (1971). The Transparent Self (rev. edition). New York.
20. Altman,I.,& Taylor,D.A.(1973),Social Penetration,New York,Rinehart & Winston.
21. Kelly, G. A. (1955). The Psychology of Personal Constructs, New York, W. W. Norton.
22. Segraves, R. T. (1982). Marital Therapy. New York, Plenum.
23. Neimeyer, G. (1985). Personal Constructs in the Counselling of Couples (pp.201-215), in Anticipating Personal Construct Psychology. Edited by Epting, F., Landfield, A. W., Lincoln, University of Nebraska Press.
24. Frelick, L.F. & Waring, E.M. Marital Therapy in Psychiatric Practice, New York, Brunner/Mazel (1987).
25. Gottman, J.M., Silver, N. (1999). The Seven Principles for Making Marriage Work. Three Rivers Press, New York.
26. Locke , H. J., Wallace, E. M. (1959). Short Marital Adjustment and Prediction Tests: Their Reliability and Validity. Marriage and Family Living 21:251255.
27. Goldberg, D. P. (1972). Detection of Psychiatric Illness by Questionnaire, Institute of Psychiatry Maudsley Monographs No.21. Oxford, Oxford University Press, Maudsley Monograph.
28. Dinkmeyer and Carlson: Time for a Better Marriage. Impact Publishers.
29. Wesley, S. & Waring, E.M. (1996) A Critical Review of Marital Therapy Outcome Research, Canadian Psychiatric Association Journal, Vol 40, No 7.
30. Waring, E. M. & Russell, L. (1980). Cognitive Family Therapy. Journal of Sex and Marital Therapy 6(4):258-273.

31. Waring, E. M., Carver, C., Stalker, C., Fry, R. & Schaefer, B. (1990). A Randomized Clinical Trial of Cognitive Marital Therapy. Journal of Sex and Marital Therapy 16(3):165-180.

32. Waring, E. M., Carver, C., & Gitta, M. (1991). Waiting List Controlled Trial of Cognitive Marital Therapy in Severe Marital Discord. Journal of Marital and Family Therapy, 17(3):243-256.

33. Dandenau, M., Johnson, S.M. (1994). Facilitating Intimacy: A Comparative 0 Outcome Study of Emotionally Focused and Cognitive nterventions. Journal of Marital and Family Therapy, 20;17-33.

34. Waring, E. M., (1994). The Role of Marital Therapy in the Treatment of Depressed Married Women. Canadian Journal of Psychiatry, 39(8), p568- 571.

35. Waring, E. M., et al (1989). Dysthymia: Randomized Study of Cognitive Marital Therapy and Antidepressants. Psychiatry Digest, 1:1.

36. Waring , E. M., Chamberlaine, H.C., Carver, C. M. , Stalker, C. A. & Schaefer, B. (1995). A Pilot Study of Marital Therapy as a Treatment for Depression. American Journal of Family Therapy, 23(1):p3-10.

37. Waring, E. M., (1994). The Role of Marital Therapy in the Treatment of Depressed Married Women. Canadian Journal of Psychiatry, 39(8), p568- 571.

38. Waring, E. M., Schaefer, B. & Fry, R. (1994). The Influence of Therapeutic Self-Disclosure on Perceived Marital Intimacy. Journal of Sex and Marital Therapy 20(2):135-146.

Table
Time for a Better Marriage

Self-Disclosure of Personal Constructs

Edward M. Waring, M.D., D. Psych., F.R.C.P. (C), F.A.B.P.N.

Sidney Jourard's (19) description of the role of self-disclosure in marriage is reviewed. George Kelly's (20) theory of personal constructs is described in an effort to explain the complexity of successful marriages and strong families. A kind of marital therapy based on the technique of self-disclosure and the rationale that couple pathology results from erroneous personal constructs is described. The idea that these faulty schemas largely derive from the observation of and experience with one's parents' marriage is discussed. The self-disclosure of personal constructs may provide a distinctive approach to family therapy
(Fam Proc, 29:399-413, 1990).

SIDNEY JOURARD (19), in his book *The Transparent Self*, stated that a choice that confronts every one of us at every moment is this: "Shall we permit our fellow persons to know us as we are, or shall we seek instead to remain an enigma, an uncertain quality, wishing to be seen as something we are not?" (p. iii). Jourard wondered whether there was some connection between his clients' needs to consult with a professional psychotherapist and their reluctance to be known by their spouses and families.

Jourard commented that "Husbands and wives are strangers one to the other to an incredible degree" (p. 4). He described a happily married couple—something he thought was altogether rare: "They know each other, care for and about one another, respond to the needs, actions and emotions of the other, and respect each other's idiosyncrasies and uniqueness" (p. 31). He suggested that, in our society, people marry in a romantic haze, usually ignorant of the thoughts, feelings, and aims of their future spouse, partly as a result of deliberate ambiguity or contrivance on the part of the other.

Jourard's research demonstrated that women generally disclose more than men, and that female married subjects disclose more than male married subjects, and that married subjects in general disclose most to their spouse. He suggested that too much or too little self-disclosure betokens disturbance in self and in interpersonal relationships, but he did not know which was cause and which was effect, and wondered if it really mattered.

Jourard suggested that the consequence of disclosing one's inner thoughts, feelings, and wants was that one learns: 1) the extent to which one is similar to another; 2) to understand the other person's needs; and 3) the extent to which the other person accords with or deviates from one's own value system and from moral and ethical standards. He hinted that one's self-disclosing behavior might be a product of how one's childhood disclosures are met in our family of origin - some ignored, some rewarded, some punished. He suggested that in marriage one withdraws disclosure from the family of origin for increased self-disclosure with the spouse. He believed that "healthy personalities" are people who not only play their roles satisfactorily (normal people), but also derive personal satisfaction from role enactment and are able to disclose themselves in some optimum degree to at least one significant other.

Jourard even seemed to anticipate Kelly's (20) theory of personal constructs, with which, so far as I can tell, he was unfamiliar, when he wrote, "men's concepts of the subjective side of other people...are often naive, crude or downright inaccurate" (p. 51). He hinted that the aim of marital or family therapy would not be so much to remove salient concerns like persistent arguments, but to alter interpersonal behavior from the range that generates the problems (manipulating self and others) to a pattern that generates and maintains a close, confiding relationship or ends the relationship by mutual consent.

Jourard's insights that the process of self-disclosure was critical to the development of close, confiding relationships and was associated with marital adjustment have led to considerable research in the social psychology of marriage but, surprisingly, little interest by marital therapists in the possibility that specifically focusing on a spouse's self-disclosing behavior might be an effective counseling technique.

Self-disclosure is the process of revealing one's thoughts, feelings, or past experiences to another person. The exchange of information about one's inner self is considered the major process through which relationships between people develop (1). Whether variations in the process of self-disclosure play a causal role in the development of marital discord remains to be determined. The degree to which self-disclosure between partners is vital to marital functioning is more valued in upper class social groupings (21). However, a positive relationship between the amount of self-disclosure and marital satisfaction has consistently been demonstrated. For example, Davidson, Balswick, and Halverson (9) found that spouses who report more self-disclosure in their marriage tend to report greater marital adjustment. Waring and Chelune (34) found that self-disclosing behavior, as measured by the Self-Disclosure Coding System (SDCS), is a major determinant of various aspects of marital intimacy.

Similarly, reciprocity of self-disclosure between spouses has also been found to be positively associated with marital adjustment. Hansen and Schuldt (14) found that couples with discrepancies in amount of self-disclosure output reported less marital satisfaction. Davidson et al. (9) found that the greater the discrepancy in a partner's self-disclosure of feelings, the less was a spouse's perception of marital adjustment. Some research has found self-disclosure to be less strictly reciprocal, but more flexible, in well-established relationships (11).

Although breadth of self-disclosure is typically greater in the initial stage of a relationship, depth of self-disclosures increases as the relationship continues (11). Waterman (36) has reviewed studies suggesting that marital satisfaction is associated with the depth of self-disclosures and the relevance of the material. Levinger and Senn (22) have demonstrated that there is more disclosure of unpleasant feelings between unsatisfied couples. Chelune, Rosenfeld, and Waring (8) found some inequity in the disclosure patterns of distressed couples. In contrast to non-distressed spouses, clinical partners show little similarity in their disclosure patterns, and positive disclosures by one spouse lead to an increase in negative disclosures by the other. Finally, when distressed spouses make depth disclosures, their affect is at greater variance with what they reveal than among non-distressed spouses, possibly resulting in more frequent misunderstandings.

PERSONAL CONSTRUCT THEORY

George Kelly (20) defined personality as the characteristic thoughts people have in anticipating future experiences. Kelly, like Jourard, was an academic clinical psychologist, whose book, *Psychology of Personal Constructs*, first appeared in the 1950s. Kelly invited readers to look at personality in a new and different light by construing people as using their imagination to think about our human relationships and explain our experience. He suggested that thinking about the future, like an amateur scientist, was the fundamental property of being human.

Kelly's cognitive view of personality has been rescued from the obscurity of his writing style by the increased interest, in the past decade, of academic psychologists in a cognitive view of psychotherapy (3, 24). The cognitive aspects of relationship distress have also received increased recognition by a variety of professionals with an interest in understanding and treating marital discord (18).

Kelly wrote little that directly described marriage, so, to introduce his theory, I will review a chapter by Neimeyer (26), "Personal Constructs in the Counseling of Couples." Kelly's assumptions about relationships do not specify needs or rewards, as postulated by psychodynamic or behavioral theories, but he does assume that the essence of human life is the anticipation of experience. He argued that people choose those alternatives that appear to offer the greatest opportunity for developing the meaningful anticipation of events and to extend one's understanding of experience. Regarding marital relationships, Kelly observed that "a man will choose to enlarge or secure his anticipatory system" (p. 523) in an ongoing cooperation between spouses to understand the relationship. One can only enjoy the role of wife and husband if one understands the behavior of one's spouse. In the absence of sufficient understanding, marital discord is likely. Not only does misunderstanding distort interactions between spouses, it also limits the elaboration of their experience as a couple. If spouses refuse to acknowledge or accept one another's different understandings of their experience, the constant adjustment of the system, vital to successful marriage, will become static. Kelly observed, "For the more complicated interplay of roles—for example, the husband and wife interplay—the understanding...must reach at least a level of generality which will enable the participants to predict each other's behavior in situations not covered by mere household traffic rules" (p. 96). Hostility in marriage is thus viewed as both spouses insisting on maintaining certain beliefs in an effort to manipulate the other spouse into providing behavior that can be used as evidence validating the beliefs—the personal construct. Spouses in maladjusted marriages disregard, elaborate, or distort experience to maintain these static beliefs. It is likely that certain personal constructs, once firmly established, persist in the face of considerable counterevidence.

These thoughts-beliefs-schemata-personal constructs about relationships develop gradually from experience in trying to understand relevant life events. Among the most significant of these experiences is the observation of one's parents' marriage. The importance of these observations is epitomized in the dynamic concept of "marital transference neurosis" in which the explanation—the personal construct—of the parents' marital distress is used to understand the current marriage (23, 28). Therapists can assist couples to articulate change in behavior. Spouses' disclosures will produce awareness that they may not share similar understandings of presenting issues. The therapist should encourage self-disclosure of ideas about the relationship.

Segraves (30) has attempted to integrate concepts from psychodynamic, behavior, and systems theory, as applied to chronic marital discord, by employing Kelly's theory of personal constructs. From the perspective of marriage, one's behavior toward one's spouse is partially a function of one's perception of the spouse's behavior, which is related to past experience, and partially a function of the spouse's actual behavior which in part may be provoked. Segraves argues that spouses form abstractions about relationships—whether one calls these abstractions personal constructs, personifications, schemata, introject, or transference, doesn't matter. What does matter is that these ideas serve to influence future perceptions. Thus, personal constructs are concepts that are co-determined by memory, imagination, and perception of current reality, which organize one's approach to personal relationships. Segraves extends Kelly's theory to marriage by suggesting that marital discord is a consequence of a few simple, rigid, personal constructs, while intimacy occurs when partners have many, complex, flexible, personal constructs. Segraves suggests that in marital discord these faulty schemata can be altered by self-disclosure, considering alternative explanations, or experiencing the spouse's behavior as discrepant from one's expectations—an experience Kelly described as constructive alternativism.

Segraves argues that each spouse enters the marriage with certain beliefs about the form marriage should take, and about the discrepancy in these beliefs between spouses is a source of conflict while similarity in beliefs facilitates marital adjustment.

The marital therapist, according to Segraves, must realize that spouses enter therapy with different assumptions about what has caused their chronic marital discord. Thus, for spouses to feel that therapy is worthwhile, they must change their ideas about each other and about their relationship. In essence, Segraves argues that chronic marital discord is a consequence of both spouses' fixated way of misconstruing their partner's character and motivation. Schemas are modifiable by direct, personal behavioral disconfirmation as well as by the method of verbal persuasion. He reports research that describes unhappy couples as showing less interpersonal sensitivity and less self-disclosure.

Segraves suggests that personal constructs are learned from previous close relationships with the opposite sex and from observation of the marriage in the family of origin. Spouses in a disturbed marriage show a tendency to construe the spouse erroneously as similar to past figures of the opposite sex. These spouses have a relative paucity of personal constructs relevant to understanding members of the opposite sex, as well as a habitual cognitive structure that is low in cognitive complexity—often described as traits such as being rigid, insensitive, opinionated, or stubborn. These spouses ignore the subtleties of complex interactions because of a need to reduce ambiguity, uncertainty, and inconsistency.

Clinical Example

A couple with chronic marital discord participated in a therapy designed to enhance marital intimacy through the self-disclosure of personal constructs. This couple was referred by friends, who had had counseling, because they were drifting apart as well as having frequent, increasingly bitter arguments. The couple had been married for nine years and had two daughters, aged seven and four. The husband was a professional man who traveled extensively, and the wife enjoyed managing the home and raising their two daughters.

During the initial assessment, the spouses were asked for their explanations of the growing distance in their relationship. The wife attributed her withdrawal to feelings of bitterness toward her husband, which had developed after the birth of their second child. She resented her husband's frequent absences from the home, she was frightened by his increasing displays of temper, and she felt lonely because he spent less time with her as a companion.

The husband explained the drifting apart, which he agreed seemed to occur after the birth of his two daughters, as a feeling of boredom that had developed as he found his wife more preoccupied with the children and domestic details.

Asked about how they initially met and how their relationship developed, the wife revealed that they had met through her job as a secretary/receptionist in a public relations firm. She disclosed that her husband was one of many businessmen who reported through her office. She said that she was attracted to him physically and perceived him as mature and assertive in comparison to her previous boyfriends. She revealed that she thought he was married at the time they first dated. He corrected her and revealed that he was separated from his first wife when they first dated. He disclosed that he was attracted to his wife by her beauty and her pleasant manner. He stated that he remembered that his wife's parents had not been pleased when the couple started dating.

The spouses both agreed that they had a mutual interest in music and the entertainment and dining related to their professional roles. When asked about his previous marriage, the husband revealed that his first wife had been an ambitious, career-oriented woman, which meant frequent separations. A business opportunity for his wife in another city led to his decision to separate rather than follow her career goals. He acknowledged that his first wife and he had frequent differences of opinion during their three-year marriage, but they had parted on good terms. His wife revealed that she had not given much thought to why her husband's previous marriage had failed. She said that her decision to date a man she thought was married was in part motivated by rebellion against her parents' values.

They spontaneously disclosed that they had broken up after six months of courtship when she discovered he had been dating another woman. He reported that this occurred as a reaction to frequent arguments they had about making a commitment to marriage. They both reported having had romances during this three-month separation, which ended when he called her again. They both denied any feelings of jealousy or bitterness about these short-lived romances.

He revealed that he construed his parents' marriage as being quite poor, which he believed was due to his father's bad temper. He disclosed that his mother, as well as his brother and sister, had experienced verbal and physical abuse. He recalled that his parents had separated briefly twice during his childhood. He did not feel close to his family and he actively avoided visits or contact.

She described her parents' marriage as good. However, she perceived that her mother had been excessively involved with her, which she explained was because she was an only child. She revealed that her mother was always trying to please everybody, including her father, whom she perceived as a very private man. She added that she suspected her father might have had an affair. They both agreed that their first few years of marriage had been quite happy. Although he reported feeling lonely and bored at times on the road, these frequent separations were not particularly upsetting. They enjoyed an active social life when together. She spent considerable time with her parents when he was away on business.

The births of their two daughters were planned, and they were both very pleased. She left work and devoted her time to the children. He was not so comfortable with his role as a father. She disclosed that she found his family difficult to deal with, and he revealed that he found his mother-in-law quite intrusive.

They indicated that they were committed to the relationship and wanted to see the marriage improve. They agreed that since the arguments they both had expressed less affection. The couple also agreed that she was more disclosing of thoughts and feelings than he was. They repeated that difference of opinion frequently led to arguments in which he occasionally lost his temper. He felt that he was not a good listener at home because he had to listen as part of his job and was often tired and frustrated after work. She said that she enjoyed conversations with her husband, but was a bit of a mind-reader. They agreed that their sexual relationship was good. They felt their relationships as a couple with friends, children, and extended family were good except for his continuing turmoil with his parents. They believed they were quite compatible regarding goals, values, and interests.

I suggested to them that their loss of closeness might be related to their inability to resolve differences of opinion that had first surfaced during their courtship and dominating. The couple thought these observations were plausible, and accepted a treatment contract involving ten one-hour sessions of self-disclosure of personal constructs.

The initiation of the first therapy session with this couple will be described in order to illustrate the process of self-disclosure of personal constructs as it occurs in the course of therapy.

Therapist:	What's your explanation of why you have drifted apart as a couple?
Wife:	George refuses to accept my point of view about anything!
Therapist:	Your idea is that your drifting apart was due to your husband not respecting your opinions?
Wife:	Yes.
Therapist:	What's your theory about how you selected a man who doesn't respect your opinions?
Wife:	He wasn't that way when we met.
Therapist:	What is your explanation about why he has changed?
Wife:	He changed after the children were born. I don't know why.

Therapist:	George, what were you thinking while your wife was talking? [This standardized ques tion facilitates self-disclosure.]
Husband:	I was thinking that Alice wants me to agree with all her decisions.
Therapist:	What's your explanation of why your wife wants total consensus?
Husband:	She wants to control the kids' behavior.
Therapist:	How did you manage to pick a controlling woman?
Husband:	She always knew what she wanted, and I liked that at first because I didn't.

One can observe the process of self-disclosure commencing as the wife begins to think about her reasons for marrying a man whom she perceives as not respecting her opinions, and the husband begins to think about why he picked a woman whom he construed as controlling. Both spouses will now be exploring their own motives for spouse selection and, hopefully, with an objectivity provided by the passage of time. Both spouses can become a resource regarding observations and explanations of their own and their mate's earlier motives.

Therapist:	What were you thinking while your spouse was talking?
Wife:	I was thinking that I didn't know what I wanted as clearly as George thinks. I was pretty confused.
Therapist:	What's your theory of what was causing your confusion?
Wife:	Because of my father's affair, and I was con fused about who I could trust.
Therapist:	What's your theory of why your father had an affair?
Wife:	I don't know. He was spending a lot of time with his secretary who was a young woman. I don't know.
Therapist:	What were you thinking while your wife

	was talking?
Husband:	I think he [father-in-law] was tired of being taken for granted at home, at least that's what he told me once.
Therapist:	What's your theory about why spouses are taken for granted?

We are now a long way from the original focus of drifting apart in the present. We are now exploring reasons for an affair that occurred in the wife's parents' marriage, men being taken for granted in marriage. Perhaps we will discover that this occurred in his parents' marriage.

DISCUSSION

This approach is based on the notion that closeness between husband and wife is the single thread that explains successful marriages and strong families (32). The self-disclosure of personal constructs between spouses is a unique approach designed to enhance marital intimacy and improve marital functioning (32). A series of controlled outcome studies have demonstrated that this approach is efficient. Nine out of ten couples who are offered this approach commence the ten sessions of therapy, and eight out of ten complete the ten sessions. The approach is also effective, both subjectively and objectively. Most couples feel they have benefited from the ten sessions and therapists evaluate two-thirds as improved. Self-disclosure of personal constructs is effective in significantly reducing symptoms of distress and improving some aspects of marital quality (7, 27, 32, 33, 35). In this discussion, I wish to focus on observations and opinions about how self-disclosure of personal constructs produces therapeutic change and implications for the practice of marital and family therapy in general.

Increasing the Amount of Self-Disclosure between Spouses Good marriages are characterized by greater amounts of self-disclosure than are poor marriages. This is obviously only a description of good marriages and not necessarily an explanation of how good marriages develop. However, this approach is based on the assumption that increasing the amount of self-disclosure between spouses of their thoughts, memories, and concepts about relationships will improve toward the opposite sex occurs spontaneously as the couple gets to know each other. Marital discord may be a consequence of neurotic withholding or deliberate contrivance on the part of spouses who fail to disclose about their genuine self. When these couples are asked in therapy to disclose motives that may have been withheld for five, ten, or twenty years, these revelations may cause suffering and may stimulate one or both spouses to reevaluate their commitment to the marriage. Thus, self-disclosure of personal constructs has the potential to produce painful insights. However, this understanding allows spouses the choice of accepting the relationship as flawed, redefining the relationship on a more authentic basis, or terminating the relationship.

Self-disclosure is not self-exposure. Self-exposure in therapy involves revealing dishonest motives, feelings, or behaviors, such as confessing to marrying one's spouse to escape an unhappy home life, expressing suppressed feelings of hatred, or revealing sexual improprieties. Self-exposure produces distance and not closeness. Self-disclosure, in contrast, is revealing the reasons for one's unhappiness with one's home life, the motives behind suppressing one's feelings, or the expressing of dissatisfactions with one's marriage, which might motivate an affair.

Self-disclosure of personal constructs is not an approach for dishonest people or people who like to "let it all hang out." Self-exposure is the use of an assessment interview to reveal a secret; self-disclosure is the process of understanding how a person becomes secretive. One would hope that self-disclosure will assist spouses to reveal personal constructs that lie behind amount of self-disclosure increases, the depth of the disclosures become more personal and private. The expectations, memories, and attitudes revealed become more psychologically sophisticated.

For example, a spouse who is engaged in the process of self-disclosure may be exploring the reasons for having chosen a spouse with certain qualities. Eventually, the spouse may not be able to explain the choice because the reasons have not been consciously examined or because the constructs are beyond awareness (that is, unconscious). At this point, the therapist will ask the other spouse to assist by revealing his or her thoughts about the question, which the partner may not be able to answer. The therapist may also assist by offering several possible explanations for consideration. These techniques are designed to facilitate the amount of self-disclosure rather than to identify a specific personal construct.

Not all disclosures are constructive. There are couples who refuse to participate in self-disclosure because they find the process frightening or the disclosures disturbing. Self-disclosure that is persistently self-critical, consistently self-justifying, or expressed in a sarcastic tone, will produce distance rather than understanding. The therapist's task is to increase the amount of self-disclosure about personal experiences and motivations and to prevent the direct expression of criticism or anger toward the spouse, as well as to encourage interpersonal curiosity. Whether or not simply increasing the amount of self-disclosure between spouses can by itself produce therapeutic change is not known. In summary, increasing the amount of self-disclosure between spouses can be viewed as a technique designed to improve communication skills.

Reciprocity of Self-Disclosure Research has consistently demonstrated that marital adjustment is related to a factor described by various authors as "reciprocity," "equity," "compatibility," and "homogamy" (2, 10, 16, 25). This factor of "reciprocity" is descriptive of good relationships; while we do not know if there is a cause-and-effect relationship, the factor of reciprocity may also be descriptive of good marital therapy. Thus, the technique of self-disclosure of personal constructs has been designed to provide reciprocity of the amount, kind, and depth of self-disclosure.

Social exchange theory supports the idea that a balance in the amount of self-disclosure between partners in therapy may be necessary (16). According to social ex-change theory, we consciously review the costs and rewards of our relationships, and if the rewards outweigh the costs, the relationship will continue. Thus, reciprocity of self-disclosure can be understood as rewarding if both spouses provide explanations that help explain their discord and offer opportunity for change; revealing weaknesses and insecurities are perceived as equal costs by the couple.

Psycho-dynamically oriented therapists argue that social exchange theory is simplistic and that it minimizes the importance of unconscious factors in mate selection and in chronic marital discord. As evidence, they point to the kind of marriage in which costs obviously outweigh rewards but, for presumed unconscious reasons, the couples wish to continue their relationship in spite of obvious suffering. These relationships, suggests Willi (37), may be an example of unconscious reciprocity in which couples collude to remain at the same level of emotional immaturity. Dominion (10) has reviewed studies which suggest that couples are compatible for neuroticism (10). Thus, the therapist must allow self-disclosure sure about conflicts to be reciprocal between partners and avoid the tendency to see one spouse as "normal" and one as "abnormal"; rather, the therapist should find the personal constructs that explain the "unhealthy" collusion between the spouses.

It is possible, one supposes, that successful marriages are characterized by "unconscious" equity. Through selection of similar mates to begin with and constructive self-disclosure during courtship, these couples develop successful marriages. Couples with marital discord may select, "unconsciously," spouses with specific conflicts and, through avoidance of self-disclosure during courtship, protect their frailties and insecurities. The process of self-disclosure in these marriages may reveal equity or incompatibility for specific conflicts and insecurities. Therapy may reduce the tension produced if these frailties are projected onto the spouse.

Ego Relevance of Disclosures If increasing the amount and depth of self-disclosure in a reciprocal fashion between spouses in a disturbed marriage is a technique that will reveal conflicts and insecurities, what next? Most couples have argued about their conflicts at great length, usually with much heat and little light. Many couples have revealed to me that previous therapists allowed them to rehash the same old arguments, leading them to feel hopeless and helpless, and leading them to withdraw from therapy. These couples could disclose their attitudes about politics, religion, or nuclear war, hardly relevant to their current concerns.

Fortunately, most couples find the disclosure of their memories, attitudes, and expectations—personal constructs—about their parents' marriages as both novel and relevant to their concerns about poor communication, persistent arguments, or drifting apart. Most couples believe that ideas they have developed through observations and experience with their parents' marriages are relevant to their own discord. These personal constructs about relationships – parents, grandparents, brothers, sisters and previous relationships are viewed by couples as relevant to disclose in therapy in order to understand their current conflict. Relevance does not mean causation. Relevance suggests that couples believe that continuing to participate in a structured experience of self-disclosure about their concepts about relationships may prove therapeutic. There are, of course, a few couples who do not accept the relevance of these memories and constructs of old relationships, and this therapy is not indicated for such couples.

For the past fifteen years, I have said to hundreds of couples, "Tell me about your parents' marriage." The majority of spouses with marital discord respond that it wasn't very good! A minority respond, "They are still together. It seemed all right to me." When I ask what they mean by "all right," these spouses are often stumped. A few cannot describe their parents' marriage. Contrast these responses with those of couples from successful marriages and strong families: "They were very close"; "They liked, loved, and respected each other."

Early experience is fundamentally important to personality development. Whether or not early experience, particularly the quality of the mother-infant relationship, is a necessary or sufficient predisposing factor to adult psychopathology has been a more controversial issue. However, recent evidence has accumulated that personality is a major predisposing factor in some types of adult psychopathology—mainly nonpsychotic emotional illness (17).

The study of adult psychopathology's relationship to early experience initially associated hysterical conversion symptoms in adulthood with traumatic sexual events in childhood (12). The development of psychoanalysis depended on Freud's assertion that these traumatic events were fantasies. However, sexual abuse of children is now accepted as a predisposing factor to such disorders as borderline personality and hysterical symptoms.

Whether real or imagined, psychiatrists have continued to explore the connection between unpleasant early childhood experience—abuse, neglect, enmeshment, inconsistency, separation, and/or divorce—and various types of adult psychopathology. Gradually, psychiatry retreated from the idea of a single traumatic event to the idea of a single traumatic relationship. Bowlby's (5, 6) concepts of disturbed attachments in the mother-child relationship as predisposing factors became the focus of efforts to explain adult psychopathology.

More recently, psychiatrists have decided that perhaps they have been overly critical of mothers, and broadened the scope of early experience to include the family environment. Some aspect of this environment—as yet not clearly defined—predisposes a child to the development of behavior disorder or later adult psychopathology and marital discord.

I would like to add another perspective that may shed some light on human nature and the role of early experience in the predisposition to adult psychopathology. Relationships are the aspect of early experience most ignored by developmental psychopathologists. The mother-infant relationship has been explored; the father-child relationship investigated; the parent-child relationship is a contemporary focus. The marriage-child relationship has largely been ignored. The marriage relationship-child interaction is the neglected issue of psychological investigation.

Couples who seek help for marital maladjustment construe their parents' marriages in a negative light. When they describe what was wrong with their parents' marriage, they list physical abuse, persistent arguments, affairs, drinking, abandonment, separation, divorce, lack of affection, and incompatibility. The problems they describe in their parents' marriages are frequently mirrored in their own relationship. Schutz (29) was the first to describe that modeling or identification could occur with relationships as well as individuals. The technique of self-disclosure suggests that the experience with (feelings) and observations of (thoughts) of one's parents' marital quality may have some influence on the development of a parallel, repetitive pattern in the current marital relationship.

What is most striking, however, is that when you ask these couples for their explanation of why their parents' relationship had problems, they almost always say one of the parents was to blame! They attribute to one parent the total responsibility for the unhappy marriage they observed and experienced. Segraves (30) has identified these overly simplistic personal constructs as "shallow images" (p. 176). These spouses describe one parent as insensitive, selfish, stubborn, cold, rigid, inconsiderate. When asked how this parent came to be this way, they report they have never thought about an explanation! When asked why the other spouse might have picked such a person, they are dumfounded! These naive schemas, developed to explain painful childhood experiences, are negative, simplistic, and rigid.

Segraves suggests that couples with chronic marital discord construe their spouses inaccurately as having the same characteristics as the "blamed parent" and attribute current marital discord to these "shallow images." Our experience has been that many of these perceptions are in fact accurate—spouses may have been selected, perhaps unconsciously, for their potential for congruence with a specific personal construct. Our observation is that the explanation given by spouses to understand their parents' marital discord is the undisclosed personal construct—the naïve schema.

Psychodynamic theories have advocated the primacy of the quality of the attachment between infant and mother as the crucial predisposing factor in the development of personality and, thus, the potential for a close, confiding relationship in marriage (5, 6). Personal construct theory does not dismiss the validity of the psychodynamic hypothesis, but questions the relevance of the concept for distressed couples since so few couples are able or see the relevance of disclosing feelings from infancy. On the other hand, most couples have memories about their parents' marriage that they can recall from about the age of four or five until they finally leave home.

What appears to be most relevant to the development of a close, confiding relationship in marriage is the personal constructs children develop, between the ages of four and fifteen to explain their experience and observation of the parents' marriage (31). These thoughts are conscious and available for self-disclosure. Adolescents often report they develop cherished ideas about whom they should marry in order to prevent the suffering they observed their parents experiencing. Couples can report memories of how their parents expressed affection, if they expressed affection to one another; couples can report how their parents attempted to resolve difference of opinion, and how they communicated with each other. The adult can recall these observations, but it is obvious that, at least in our culture, many couples do not routinely share such observations. Thus, they find self-disclosure of personal constructs to be innovative, interesting, and different from their own attempts to talk about and understand their marital discord.

The child also experiences feelings of insecurity about the parents' marriage when there is tension about possible separations, problems with substance abuse, verbal, physical, or sexual abuse, and divorce.

Spouses report that this insecurity motivated the development of personal constructs that led to simple explanations- blaming one parent - and conscious decisions to avoid repeating patterns they observed in childhood. These couples are mystified when their marriages developed similar problems. Children who have had the opportunity to reveal these ideas by confiding in friends, brothers, sisters, and teachers, report the value of self-disclosure. Most couples report that if they attempted to disclose their observations about their parents' mixture of frailties to one or both parents, these disclosures were suppressed or ignored by the parents.

Responding versus Reacting to Self-Disclosure The self-disclosure of personal constructs in marital therapy can be helpful only if the spouses are available to listen, make an honest effort to understand their spouse, and do not use the disclosures in a destructive fashion once the sessions have finished. Spouses often react emotionally to disclosures that they do not wish to hear. Tears or anger can be used defensively or as a manipulation to inhibit honest disclosures during sessions. Bowen (4) has suggested that couples who cannot resolve interpersonal conflict will often involve a third party, including one's therapist, to reduce the tension that self-disclosure produces and, by stimulating the therapist to react to tears or anger, to avoid resolving the issue.

The therapist must assist both spouses to respond to the self-disclosure of personal constructs, rather than react, which inhibits understanding. The therapist assists by introducing a treatment contract in which both spouses agree not to interrupt while the other spouse is disclosing. The therapist also assists by modeling empathetic listening. The therapist also assists by asking the spouse who is listening to think of possible explanations when the other spouse is unable to disclose personal constructs. The therapist must be aware that when a spouse attempts to break the fundamental rule of not interrupting the couple may be reacting to specific constructs which may be the root of the discord.

When a therapist feels that therapy is not progressing because of the characteristics of one spouse, the therapist is *reacting* to a personal construct that attributes blame for the discord, rather than *responding* to the couple's concerns. Finally, the therapist must also respond to a spouse's sense of loss if, during the course of therapy, a cherished personal construct is changed, which often makes the spouse feel foolish that a misconstruing of the other spouse's character or motives has contributed to the marital discord.

While self-disclosure of personal constructs forces spouses to reveal their own thoughts, and while this minimizes the self-justification and projection so common in marital discord, the therapist must also respond to the couple's increasing under-standing of fundamental incompatibilities that may be revealed for the first time. The therapist must encourage responding by allowing both spouses to disclose their thoughts about separation if this is an issue, and prevent their reacting to threats of separation. While this discussion is theoretical, research has demonstrated that teaching couples empathetic listening skills, independent of the content, is an effective form of marital therapy (15).

CONCLUSIONS

The self-disclosure of personal constructs would appear to be an effective and efficient technique for reducing symptoms of nonpsychotic emotional illness and improving some aspects of marital functioning. The technique is not indicated for couples with major affective disorder or substance-abuse problems.

Couples who accept the technique usually complete ten sessions of therapy and usually report subjective improvement, which they attribute to increased understanding and improved communication. If we view the technique as enhancing relationships by maximizing empathy and self-disclosure as a basic communication skill, the technique and its effectiveness are remarkably similar to that described in previous research (13). Kelly's (20) goal was not to solve the problems of the couples but, rather, to provide couples with skills they could use both to solve and prevent future problems in their relationships, to minimize misconceptions and friction, and to achieve high levels of understanding, harmony, and intimacy. But where does this leave the theory of personal constructs? Do simple, naive, rigid constructs cause marital discord?

Couples seldom report that they have altered some idea that they had about their spouse. Is therapeutic change really a consequence of the disclosure of personal constructs or alterations of personal constructs? Are these concepts more important to therapists than to couples? Is outcome determined by the development of self-disclosure skills, or is what is disclosed also important? What personal constructs, if any, are most relevant to marital discord and where do they come from? Does "constructive alternativism" take more than ten sessions?

Clinical experience with couples who have participated in Enhancing Marital Intimacy Therapy suggests some possibilities. Most couples with marital discord have observed and experienced poor relationships during childhood and adolescence. They almost invariably construe these problems as caused by one parent's traits or behavior. They frequently have no explanation of the dynamics of this behavior, but felt the suffering they attribute to their families of origin.

Clearly, the role of personal constructs in marital therapy needs to be studied more directly. Two possible directions are to measure personal constructs directly before and after therapy and evaluate whether alterations have occurred. Technically this is feasible using techniques such as the repertory grid (20).

Second, more direct measures of the constructs that children develop in response to marital discord should be directly studied and prospectively evaluated to identify the influence on personality and relationship development. While most couples accept the relevance of these observations for therapy, it is not yet clear whether they are really meaningful. The kind, number, and flexibility of personal constructs in marital maladjustment deserve further study.

In summary, a technique that involves the reciprocal self-disclosure of personal constructs about relationships has been demonstrated to be effective in the treatment of some, but not all kinds of chronic marital discord. The effectiveness may be due to the process of self-disclosure alone. The disclosure of beliefs about relationships may simply make the disclosure relevant to couples, thus increasing compliance. However, the technique itself may allow for observations about the relationship of specific personal constructs to specific kinds of marital discord. While couples do not attribute therapeutic success to altered beliefs, the possibility remains that constructive alternativism has occurred. The study of personal constructs directly as they relate to marital maladjustment seems indicated.

References

1. Altman,I.,& Taylor,D.A. Social Penetration:The Development of Interpersonal Relationships.New York: Holt,Rinehart & Winston,1973
2. Beavers,W.R. Successful Marriage: A family systems approach to couples therapy.New York: W.W.Norton, 1985.
3. Beck,A,T. Cognitive Therapy and the emotional disorders. New York: International Universities Press, 1976.
4. Bowen, M. Family therapy after twenty years. In S. Arieti (ed.), American hand-book of psychiatry, Vol. 5. New York: Basic Books, 1975.
5. Bowlby, J. The nature of the child's tie to his mother. International Journal of Psychoanalysis 39: 350-372, 1958.
6. _____. The role of childhood experience in cognitive disturbance. In M.J. Mahoney & A. Freeman (eds.), Cognition and psychotherapy. New York: Plenum Press, 1985.
7. Carver, C.M., Waring, E.M., Chamberlaine, C.H., McCrank, E.W., Stalker, C., & Fry, R. Detection of depression in couples in conflict. Canada's Mental Health 35(4): 1-5, 1985.
8. Chelune, G.J., Rosenfeld, L.B., & Waring, E.M. Spouse disclosure patterns in distressed and non-distressed couples. American Journal of Family Therapy 13: 24-32, 1985.
9. Davidson, B., Blaswick, J., & Halverson, C. Affective self-disclosure and marital adjustment: A test of equity theory. Journal of Marriage and the Family 45: 93-102, 1983.
10. Dominion, J. Definition and extent of marital pathology. British Medical Journal 2: 478-479, 1979.
11. Fitzpatrick, M.A. Marriage and verbal intimacy. In V.J. Derlega & J.H. Berg (eds.), Self-disclosure: Theory, research, and therapy. New York: Plenum Press, 1987.
12. Freud, S. The standard edition of the complete psychological works of Sigmund Freud, Volume II (1893-1895): Studies on Hysteria

(translator, James Strachey). London: The Hogarth Press, 1975.

13. Guerney, B.G. Relationship enhancement. San Francisco: Jossey-Bass, 1977.

14. Hansen, J.E., & Schuldt, W.J. Marital self-disclosure and marital satisfaction. Journal of Marriage and the Family 46: 923-926, 1984.

15. Harrell, J., & Guerney, B.G. Jr. Training married couples in conflict Negotiation skills. In D.h.L. Olsen (Ed.), Treating Relationships. Lale Mills IA: Graphic, 1976.

16. Hatfield, E., & Walster, G.W. A new look at love. Reading MA: Addison-Wesley, 1981.

17. Henderson, S. A development in social psychiatry: The systematic study of social bonds. Journal of Nervous and Mental Disease 168(2): 63-69, 1980.

18. Jacobson, N.S., & Margolin, G. Marital therapy: Strategies based on social learning and behavior exchange principles. New York: Brunner/Mazel, 1979.

19. Jourard, S.M. The transparent self (rev. ed.). New York: Van Nostrand Reinhold, 1971.

20. Kelly, G.A. The psychology of personal constructs. New York: W.W. Norton, 1955

21. Komarvosky, I. Blue collar marriage. New York: Random House, 1964.

22. Levinger, G., & Senn, D.J. Disclosure of feelings in marriage. Merrill Palmer Quarterly 13: 237-249, 1967.

23. Martin, P. A marital therapy manual. New York: Brunner/Mazel, 1976.

24. Meichenbaum, D. Cognitive-behavior modification: An integrative approach. New York: Plenum Press, 1977.

25. Murstein, B.I. Love, sex, and marriage through the ages. New York: Springer, 1974.

26. Neimeyer, G. Personal constructs in the counseling of couples. In F. Epting & A.W. Landfield (eds.), Anticipating personal construct psychology. Lincoln: University of Nebraska Press, 1985.

27. Russell, A., Russell, L., & Waring, E.M. Cognitive family therapy: A preliminary report. Canadian Journal of Psychiatry 25: 64-67, 1980.

28. Sager, C.J. Marriage contracts and couple therapy. New York: Brunner/Mazel, 1976.

29. Schutz, W. The interpersonal underworld. Palo Alto CA: Science and Behavioral Books, 1966.

30. Segraves, R.T. Marital therapy. New York: Plenum Press, 1982.

31. Waring, E.M. Facilitating marital intimacy through self-disclosure. American Journal of Family Therapy 9(4): 33-42, 1981

32. _____. Enhancing marital intimacy through facilitating cognitive self-disclosure. New York: Brunner/Mazel, 1988.

33 _____. Chamberlaine, C.H., McCrank, E.W., Stalker, C.A., Carver, C., Fry, R., & Barnes, S. Dysthymia: A randomized study of cognitive marital therapy and antidepressants. Canadian Journal of Psychiatry 33: 96-99, 1988.

34. _____, & Chelune, G.J. Marital intimacy and self-disclosure. Journal of Clinical Psychology 39: 183-190, 1983.

35. _____, & Russell, L. Cognitive family therapy. Journal of Sex & Marital Therapy 6: 258-273, 1980.

36. Waterman, J. Self-disclosure and family dynamics. In G. Chelune (ed.), The anatomy of self-disclosure. San Francisco: Jossey-Bass, 1980.

37. Willi, J. Couples in collusion. New York: Jason Aronson, 1982.

*Originally published in Family Process, December 1990, Vol. 29, No.4.